Project Manager's Spotlight on

Change Management

CLAUDIA BACA, PMP

HARBOR LIGHT PRESS™

San Francisco   London

Publisher: Neil Edde
Acquisitions Editors: Heather O'Connor, Maureen Adams
Developmental Editor: Maureen Adams
Production Editor: Rachel Gunn
Technical Editor: Linda Zaval
Copyeditor: Rebecca Rider
Compositor: Maureen Forys, Happenstance Type-O-Rama
Graphic Illustrator: Jeffrey Wilson, Happenstance Type-O-Rama
Proofreaders: Jim Brook, Nancy Riddiough, Amy McCarthy
Indexer: Nancy Guenther
Book Designer: Maureen Forys, Happenstance Type-O-Rama
Cover Designer and Illustrator: Daniel Ziegler, Ziegler Design

Library of Congress Card Number: 2005920768

ISBN: 0-7821-4410-1

Manufactured in the United States of America

10 9 8 7 6 5 4 3 2 1

Project Manager's Spotlight on

Change Management

About the Author

Claudia Baca has been active in the project management industry since 1984 and has experience in the information technology, telecommunications, and e-commerce industries. During her varied career, Claudia has managed many mission critical projects for a major telecommunications company and several Internet companies. Currently, Claudia is the Vice President of Consulting Services with QuantumPM. She lectures and teaches for the Project Management Institute's Denver chapter as well as for Colorado State University. Claudia was a member of the leadership team that produced the standard for Project Management Maturity, OPM3. In addition, she has a Master's Certificate in Program Management from Denver University. She earned her PMP in 1995 and was recertified in 2001 and 2004.

Claudia also has much experience writing and editing. She is a coauthor of the paper "Organizational Project Management Maturity Model (OPM3)" presented at the PMI Global Congress Europe, 2003. She also coauthored the "The Past, the Present and the Future of OPM3" presented at the PMI Global Congress North America, 2004. In addition, she is the technical editor of the *PMP: Project Management Professional Study Guide* and the *IT Project+ Study Guide* and is the coauthor of *PMP: Project Management Professional Workbook*, all published by Sybex.

To our valued readers,

Harbor Light Press was created as an imprint of Sybex, Inc. to help business professionals acquire the practical skills and knowledge they need to meet today's most pressing business challenges.

Our books serve the people responsible for getting the job done—project managers charged with delivering a product on time and under budget; human resource directors faced with a complex array of resource decisions; support staff determined to exceed the goals set for them; and others who recognize that great business plans are only as good as the people who implement and manage them.

Harbor Light Press is committed to publishing authoritative, reliable, yet engaging business books written by authors who are outstanding instructors and experienced business professionals. The goal for all of our books is to connect with our readers, to understand their needs, and to provide them with solutions that they can put to use immediately.

Neil Edde
Publisher
Harbor Light Press

To my family

Contents

Foreword

The Project Manager's Spotlight Series is written for those of you who are engaged in projects at the day-to-day level of business. You're working on projects such as server consolidation, piloting new products in the marketplace, or opening a new branch or storefront. These day-to-day projects keep businesses moving forward, carving out market share, meeting strategic goals, and improving the firm's bottom line. These projects, while vitally important to the companies you work for, are not necessarily multi-million dollar, multi-year projects that require meticulous disciplines and precise methodologies.

The Project Manager's Spotlight Series shows you the how-to's of project management on a practical level. These books help you apply solid principles of project management without the rigor. You'll find tools, tips, and techniques to help you use Project Management Institute–based practices in your small- to medium-sized projects; these are tips you can read over the weekend and be ready and able to apply on Monday morning.

—Kim Heldman

Acknowledgments

There are many people I would like to thank for their efforts on this book. First and foremost, I couldn't have put this book together without the support and help of the professionals at Sybex who dedicated a lot of their effort and patience.

More specifically, I would like to thank Heather O'Connor, acquisitions editor, and Kim Heldman, my guardian angel throughout this entire process, who both conceived the book as part of the new *Spotlight on Project Management* series. As a current project manager and a teacher of basic project management courses, I was very excited by the idea of this book. I realized how I had struggled through the years to make change management work for me and felt I had hints and tricks that I could share. Without Heather and Kim's ideas, enthusiasm, and willingness to work with my ideas, this book simply wouldn't exist.

I also send many thanks to my second acquisitions editor, Maureen Adams, who took over for Heather. Her wisdom and guidance kept the book on track. I really appreciated her laborious efforts to make this book shine. Also thanks to Rachel Gunn, production editor, and Rebecca Rider, copyeditor, who took my words and made them better in every way. In addition, special thanks to my technical editor Linda Zaval, and again to Kim Heldman for checking my facts and providing additional ideas. This book also required some artwork to be rendered and I appreciate the work of Jeffrey Wilson.

And finally I'd like to thank my family for their love, understanding, and patience as I pursue my passion, project management.

Introduction

This book has been written with you, the project managers of small- to medium-sized projects, in mind. You're the ones who need just the right amount of project management skills applied to your projects. You don't need too much rigor; instead, you need just the right amount.

This book shows you how to build an effective change management system from scratch—a system that is effective enough to cover what needs to be controlled without burdening you with too much process. You also learn how to plan your change management system including the roles and responsibilities of each member of the team. In this book, I build a process flow that covers every step you need to have in place in order to be successful.

Last but not least, I spend some time on the nuances of change management—basically, the things that can go wrong when you receive lots of change requests. You'll find real world hints and tips tucked into every portion of this book. These are drawn from my 20 years of project management experience.

Use this book to set up your own change management system. Once you start seeing some success in this area, you can also use this book as a reference or a troubleshooting guide for the change management problems you encounter. I've tried to cover lots of real world scenarios that will help you through the maze of change management problems. Most of all, I hope this book gives you the fundamentals you need to deliver your project.

The Spotlight Series

The *Spotlight Series* is designed to give you practical, real life information on specific project management topics such as risk, project planning, and change management. Many times, the theory of these processes makes sense when you're reading about them, but when it's time to implement, you're left scratching your head wondering exactly how to go about it. The books in this series are intended to help you put project processes and methodologies into place on your next project without any guesswork. The authors of this series have worked hard to anticipate the kinds of questions project managers might ask, and they explain their topics in a step-by-step approach so that you can put what you've read into practice.

If you find that the topic of project management interests you, I strongly recommend that you consider becoming a certified Project Management Professional (PMP) through the Project Management Institute. They are the de facto standard in project management methodologies. You'll find many organizations now require a PMP certification for project management jobs. For more information on this topic and to help prepare you for this exam, read Kim Heldman's book, *PMP: Project Management Professional Study Guide, Second Edition.* Another helpful book to prepare you for the PMP exam is the *PMP: Project Management Professional Workbook* by this author and Patti Jansen.

What This Book Covers

This book provides a solid foundation on the concepts around change management or as it's sometimes called, change control. The current *Guide to the Project Management Body of Knowledge* (available from the Project Management Institute's bookstore at www.pmi.org) states that you should have a change control system in place. This book tells you *what* to put in place as well as *how* to make it successful. The book is organized as follows:

Chapter 1 This chapter covers the fundamentals of change management including the purpose of change management and its definition. Here, I establish the vocabulary of change management that I use throughout the rest of the book. Finally I talk about project and product lifecycles and how change management is applied to these.

Chapter 2 In this chapter, we start by discussing the roles and responsibilities of the people who work with and around a change management system. I then cover what elements of a project get controlled. After that, we spend some time on the sequence of change management and how you plan for the changes you'll face.

Chapter 3 This entire chapter deals with the process of change management. It builds a process flow one step at a time, explaining each step in length. Throughout, you will find hints and tips to apply as you design your change management system.

Chapter 4 We continue building on our process flow in this chapter by dealing with the output of a change management process. We also spend some time dealing with process exceptions and process escalations.

Chapter 5 In this chapter, we discuss what I call the incremental effect—namely, how the addition of change requests affects your overall project goals. This chapter is loaded with tips and tricks to help you deal with real world problems when things start to go wrong.

Chapter 6 In this chapter, I cover the documentation you need to effectively manage change. I talk about what forms you need, what tracking you need to implement, and what type of data you should gather.

Appendices You'll find the appendices packed with good information. We cover the fundamentals of the *PMBOK Guide* in Appendix A and the basics of critical path analysis in Appendix C. Both are provided in case you need more in-depth information on these subjects. Appendix B covers templates discussed throughout the book. I have provided a change request form and a change request log for you to use and modify for your own projects. I have also included a complete change management process flow for you to use in building your own process.

I sincerely hope the *Project Manager's Spotlight on Change Management* becomes your favorite reference book on project management tools and techniques. May you have many years of successful projects!

CHAPTER 1

Managing Project Change

A mysterious element affects every project and yet it is not often planned for. What is this phenomenon? Some call it Murphy's Law. Some call it scope creep. Some call it change. Whatever you call it, you can employ tools and techniques to help you manage it to the benefit of your project. This book provides you with the ins and outs of successful change management.

I start this chapter by relating the basics of change management. I then cover the definition of and the purpose of change management. Following this, I explain some of the common terms used in change management as well as how change management is referenced in generally accepted project management principles. Lastly, I talk about project and product lifecycles.

At the conclusion of this chapter, I introduce a case study that you can follow throughout the book. You'll get a chance to witness a project manager deal with the concepts I introduce in each chapter.

Change Management Defined

Change is inevitable and most of us project managers deal with more than our share of it on our projects. Most of us tend to think of change in terms of problems or negative consequences. Although it's true that change can be bad, it can also be good.

For example, think of a project at a major manufacturing plant. This plant hires a consulting firm to help design a new product. Halfway through the construction process, the plant requests a set of changes, but because they just asked for more product functionality, they are willing to spend more money. In this case, I bet the consulting company loves change.

Right now, you might be asking yourself why this last example constituted a change. It's time to clarify what I mean when I refer to change management and get clear about what change management is or, as it's sometimes called, *change control*.

How would you define change management? First let me explain that there are really three different elements to change management.

1. The first element of change management deals with the authority level of the project manager. You need to make sure that you have the authority to approve and deny changes that impact your project.

2. The second element of change management involves setting up an environment that fosters good change management. You need to communicate with the entire project team to set expectations on how changes on the project are to be handled.

3. The third element of change management involves setting up a system that helps you determine that a change has been requested. This system also helps you decide if you should make the change and allows you to track the change regardless of whether it is approved or denied. This system should also be comprehensive enough allow for exceptions like the following: What do you do with escalations? How do you handle people who won't follow the rules? and so on.

If you take these three elements into account, you could define *change management* as the proactive identification and management of modifications to your project.

Why Bother with Change Management?

I've known a couple of project managers who did not bother to set up a change management system on their projects. The first was barraged with requests from the client organization. She accepted all of the requests believing that she was keeping the client happy. Her good intentions actually kept her from delivering on time and within budget—she was about six months late and well over budget. When the project was complete, she had to review all of the project's problems in a project review meeting. This turned out to be grueling. It was determined by her senior management that her project management style was too loose and amiable. She was banned from managing projects of that magnitude again until she improved her results. Instead of being a hero, she ended up with a letter of reprimand in her personnel file.

The other project manager also decided that he did not need a change management process. Instead he just said no to every change that came his way. He was about four months into his project before the company replaced him. The clients and team members found him hard to work with and thought he was more concerned with finishing the project than making sure that the project he delivered was the right product for the company.

I know these examples really depict the ultimate extremes of the change management spectrum—there are millions of situations in between these. What typically happens to a project manager may simply be the result of not taking a change seriously. For instance, the project manager may approve a small change that ends up slipping the end date of the project. Without good change management in place, you are depending on luck, overtime, and your own personal power to deliver the project. In the end, you may end up drawing on all of these anyway, but you only want to use them when you have an emergency, not because you failed to plan for changes.

The bottom line then is that change is one of those necessary evils you must manage and manage well if you want to deliver on time, on budget, and with the quality defined by the client. Now let's move on and talk some more about change management definitions.

NOTE   Managing project changes well leads to projects that are on time, on budget, and within defined quality guidelines.

Let's Set Some Context

You may not be familiar with the term change management. Instead, you may have seen the terms change control, change management system, and so on. Well, they all mean the same thing—the process that is used to control project changes.

Change management is an integral part of the generally accepted principles covered in the *PMBOK Guide* . If you need a refresher on the project management processes and knowledge areas, refer to Appendix A of this book.

If you check the glossary of this guide you will not find the term change management. This is because change management is a widely known term in the project management field that refers to the overarching system that manages change (*system* here means an assemblage of processes, forms, and possibly software). You will, however, find the term control used throughout the *PMBOK Guide* and defined in its glossary. You'll also find the term change control in the five major project management process groups as well as mentioned in several of the project management knowledge areas.

Table 1.1 shows the intersection between processes and the knowledge areas; this highlights the areas concerned with change management. You'll also find this diagram in Appendix B for your future use.

You'll notice that Table 1.1 shows the abbreviation T&T. This stands for Tool and Technique. That phrase is used in the *PMBOK Guide* to denote a commonly accepted practice that is used in a process to get the results you are expecting. Change management is just that—a tool that you use to manage change.

NOTE   In case you are new to project management, check out the ANSI standard on project management, *A Guide to the Project Management Body of Knowledge, 2000 Edition*, by the Project Management Institute. www.pmi.org

TABLE 1.1: Project processes, knowledge areas, and the emphasis on change management

	INITIATING	PLANNING	EXECUTING	CONTROLLING	CLOSING
Integration		1 planning process	1 executing process	Integrated Change Control T&T: Change Control System	
Scope	1 initiating process	2 planning processes		2 controlling processes, one that deals with change management: Scope Change Control T&T: Scope Change Control	
Time		4 planning processes		Schedule Control T&T: Schedule Change Control System	
Cost		3 planning processes		Cost Control T&T: Cost Change Control System	
Procurement		2 planning processes	3 executing processes		1 closing process
Quality		1 planning process	1 executing process	1 controlling process	
Human Resource		2 planning processes	1 executing process		
Communications		1 planning process	1 executing process	1 controlling process	1 closing process
Risk		5 planning processes		1 controlling process	

The Controlling Processes

After reviewing Appendix A, you know that there are five major process groups executed during a project. In real life, Project Managers use these process groups to successfully start a project, plot the project activities, direct the project activities while they are being performed, and finally, complete the project. We undertake projects to satisfy the goals that the stakeholders determined during the project initiation.

That fourth process group, *controlling processes*, relates directly to our work here in change management. This controlling process group is concerned with monitoring and regulating the activities of the project to ensure that the goals of the project are met. This monitoring and regulating produces information that you can measure to see what variances have occurred. Once you understand that variances have occurred, you can take corrective action to keep your project on track to meet the project's objectives. We will set up our change management system in this book using these fundamentals of the controlling process group.

Within the controlling process group, you'll find four specific processes that each touch on a subject area concerning change management. Let's look at each of these subject areas:

Scope   When you are determining the *scope* of the project, you take the goals and objectives the stakeholders determine and transform them into a scope document.

The word *transform* is sometimes used interchangeably with the term *progressive elaboration*. Basically you take a concept and build upon it to create a project that delivers what the client requested.

At the beginning of the project, you take the objectives of the clients and build upon those objectives to create a *scope statement*. This scope statement should lay out exactly what the point of the project is. Most of the time, this statement is created in broad terms that can act as a litmus test for those creating the product of the project. The scope statement also sets the basis for future project decisions—a place to compare back to so you can determine what is in scope and out of scope.

An effective way to determine the scope is to define both what is included and what is excluded in your project. Imagine that you are on a project where a handheld device is being created to speed appointment information to a telephone installer. Your scope statement might say, "The device must weigh less than two pounds." This is an inclusive statement. Another way to be clear about the intention of the handheld device might be an exclusion statement such as this: "The handheld device cannot have wires connecting it to any device or power source." In this statement, you make it clear that the product must be light-weight and completely portable.

When creating the scope of the project, you need a process to control the scope once it has been set. Its purpose is to manage any changes to the project's scope. This process is really what I spend the rest of this book talking about. In essence, I am referring to the change management of the scope statement.

NOTE   A scope statement documents what is included in the project and sets the basis for future project decisions.

Time   When you are determining how long a project will take, you are working with the subject area of *time*. This area concerns the processes that ensures that the project is completed in the agreed-upon timeframe.

In this set of processes, you determine what tasks need to be completed and in what sequence. You then determine what the duration is for each task of the project. If you add up the duration for each task along the critical path, you can then determine the schedule for the project. The schedule sets the basis for future project decisions regarding the timing of the project. It provides you with a place to compare back to to determine where the project should be at any point in time.

When the schedule is set, you need to control it. *Schedule control* involves managing any changes that might affect the project schedule.

Cost   When you talk about the money associated with completing a project, you're talking about *cost management*. In this set of processes, you determine what resources will be used to complete each task of the schedule. Remember, in this context, *resources* refer to people or materials (gas, water, electricity, etc.) or equipment (backhoe, printer, post-hole digger, etc.). You determine the cost of each resource.

Once you know what resource is attributed to what piece of the work and how much that resource costs, you can then derive the budget of the project. The output of the cost budgeting process is a *cost baseline*. The cost baseline sets the basis for the overall cost of the project. Again you can compare back to this figure to determine what the project costs should be at any point in time.

Once the budget is set, you need to control it so your project completes on budget. *Cost control* involves managing and controlling any of the costs on the project.

Contract   When you're planning your project, you may find that you need to bring in outside goods or services to complete your project to the *triple constraints*—the project needs to be on time, on budget, and built to the defined quality standards.

When you procure these goods and services, you are creating a *contract* to cover both the buyer and the seller. This contract sets the basis for the relationship with the seller including all of the terms and conditions for what is being purchased, when it is purchased, and how much it costs.

You need to monitor adherence to the contract and control any changes to what has been agreed upon. In some organizations, you'll be working closely with a contract administrator or a procurement group. These are the folks who actually change the contract.

Project and Product Lifecycles

We need to talk for a minute about *lifecycles*. In other words, what are the stages of development that a project normally goes through to reach completion? A lifecycle depicts the phases of work to be accomplished. Companies use the lifecycle to depict handoffs between organizations or changes in focus for the work.

Let's be clear about two different types of lifecycles: a *project management lifecycle* and a *product development lifecycle*.

Project management lifecycle You've already heard about a project management lifecycle since you've already seen the five major process groups described in the *PMBOK Guide*. If you take these processes, which sometimes overlap or might be done in parallel, and lay them out as a lifecycle, you have what is depicted in Figure 1.1. Here you can see that very little time is actually spent in the initiating and closing processes. Most of the work on a project is done during the planning and executing/controlling phases.

FIGURE 1.1: Project management lifecycle

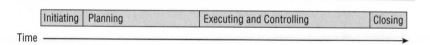

Product development lifecycle The other lifecycle you need to be aware of is the lifecycle that is used to create products at your company. Depending on the type of company, you might be using a System Development Life Cycle (SDLC) for Information Technology projects, a construction lifecycle; a defense acquisition lifecycle; a pharmaceuticals development lifecycle; and so on.

Remember that the lifecycle is completely dependent on the industry and product that you are creating. The lifecycle can be very specific or generic depending on your process. Figure 1.2 shows a generic product development lifecycle.

FIGURE 1.2: Generic product development lifecycle

Feasibility	Requirements	Design	Construction	Testing	Turnover

Time ──→

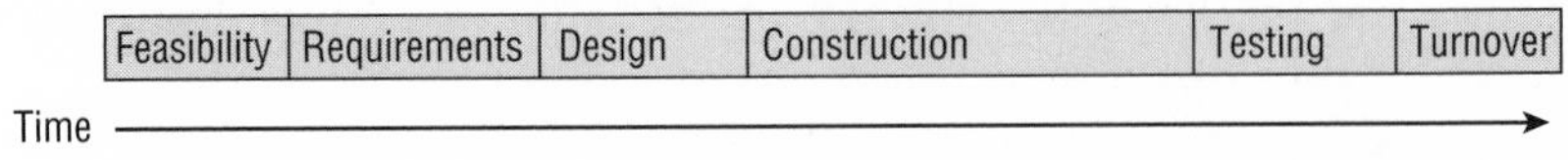

You need to understand these lifecycle concepts because you'll use them when we build our own change management system in Chapter 3 and discuss the outputs of that process in Chapter 4.

Case Study

Chris Baxter is a new project manager recently hired at RemotesUS, Inc., a subsidiary of a major Chinese manufacturer of remote controls. RemotesUS is small company that sells and distributes the Chinese remotes in the United States. So far, the company has been fairly successful and has major contracts with two of the leading cable companies. RemotesUS boasts that one out of five households in the U.S. has one of their remotes.

Chris has managed a few small projects since she was hired and is now ready for a meaty assignment. Ruth Brownstone, the CEO of RemotesUS, has called Chris into her office to explain Chris's next assignment. It seems that the parent company has created a new remote device with an artificial intelligence chip; this one device could potentially replace all electronic remotes in a consumer's house. Needless to say, the parent company is very excited about this new product and is building a major marketing campaign to launch it. The parent company also told Ruth that sales in the U.S. have not been as good as they expected. RemotesUS must do better or the parent company will look for a different sales and distribution firm to acquire in the U.S and will close RemotesUS.

While Ruth has been talking, Chris has been conjuring up visions of what a tremendous project they must have in mind for her. Most of Chris's experience has been with small to medium projects, but she feels she is ready for a big project; however, taking on a project that has the fate of the company riding on it seems a bit much.

Ruth continues her explanation, telling Chris what she has in mind for the new project—an all hands meeting. An all hands meeting? This is not exactly what Chris has in mind, but she listens on.

Ruth has decided that it is time to bring the entire company together for a couple of different reasons. First, to introduce the new product, to get them trained, and especially to get everyone excited about the product. Second, to get everyone pointed in the right direction and to make sure everyone is motivated to keep this company going. Ruth also mentions that the department heads will probably want some time set aside to meet with all of their folks in department meetings. In addition, Ruth doesn't want to hear any complaints that this meeting was a waste of anyone's time.

Ruth stresses to Chris that because of their financial shape, they can only afford to spend $50,000 for this entire meeting. Because the company has personnel in six different states and Canada, Ruth doesn't care where the meeting is held as long as it costs less than $50,000. The other major requirement that Ruth stresses is that the meeting can only last three business days. The company can't afford to have people not doing their regular jobs for more than three days. Ruth has one other demand. She says, "Oh, and by the way, make sure the meeting happens by October because the holidays will be busy and we want to make sure this product is launched in time for holiday buying."

Chris has been taking notes this entire time and thinks she is clear on the expectations of the CEO. Ruth asks Chris if she has any questions. Chris doesn't at this time. Ruth tells Chris that the rest of the specifics for the meeting should be determined by the department heads and then asks Chris to come see her when the plan is set.

Chris tells Ruth she'll be back to review the plan as soon as she can, knowing how important this assignment is to Ruth. Chris goes back to her desk disappointed with the size of the project, she doesn't think she'll be challenged by this project. But she figures she can probably handle another project or two while she is working on this one. But being the professional that she is, she dives into the planning.

The first area Chris examines is getting requirements from each of the department heads. Chris provides some insights into the structure of each department, which are depicted in Figure 1.3.

FIGURE 1.3: RemotesUS organizational chart

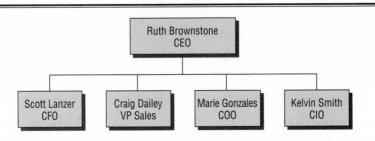

Scott Lanzer: CFO Scott's organization is rather small, but they have a lot of influence within the organization. They process all of the expense reports for the whole company and therefore, they talk to almost everyone. Chris knows that if they are happy, then they will influence others in the company. This group is located at the company headquarters.

Craig Dailey: VP Sales Craig's group is dispersed across the county. Chris hasn't had much interaction with this group, but she knows that these folks are motivated by their sales commissions and will be excited about the potential of this new product.

Marie Gonzales: COO Marie's department is very interesting because the majority of the company employees report to her. Her primary functions are shipping and receiving, as well as managing the warehouses. Most of her department is located at headquarters, but she also has people located on either coast at the warehouses. Chris has never met some of the people in Marie's department and worries about their interest in the new product.

Kelvin Smith: CIO Kelvin's department is a group of highly specialized technicians who support the entire company with technology solutions. These people will be instrumental in any technology issues that come up for the meeting.

Chris decides that she will meet one on one with each department head and find out how they would like to build their requirements for the meeting. She also decides that she'll ask for a representative from each department to be part of her project team.

Chris has one more detail that she wants to have clear in her mind before she starts laying out the project plan and schedule. She has been a fairly successful project manager before and knows she needs to define the phases or lifecycle for this project. She's decided to use a standard project management lifecycle that's based on the *PMBOK Guide* (see Figure 1.1).

The product development lifecycle for this project may be very different, though. Chris doesn't think that the product development lifecycle used by the manufacturing plant in China will work. She's also seen the system development lifecycle used in IT. That probably won't work either because her project isn't like migrating the team to a new technology. Because this project is very different, she decides she needs to design a specific lifecycle for it. She'll use the other lifecycles as guides for what this project needs.

So for this project, she decides she needs these five phases:

1. **Requirements:** In this phase, she'll spend time with each department head and find out their expectations and requirements for the meeting.

2. **Design:** Chris and the team will design the agenda and logistics for the meeting.

3. **Build:** Chris and the team will actually put all of the design in place for the meeting. The agenda will be created, flights booked, and so on.

4. **Event:** This is the actual time frame in which the event happens.

5. **Feedback:** Chris plans after-the-event discussions to verify that everyone felt that the all hands meeting was not a waste of time (to meet one of Ruth's requirements).

Chris's event planning lifecycle is depicted in Figure 1.4.

FIGURE 1.4: Chris's event planning lifecycle

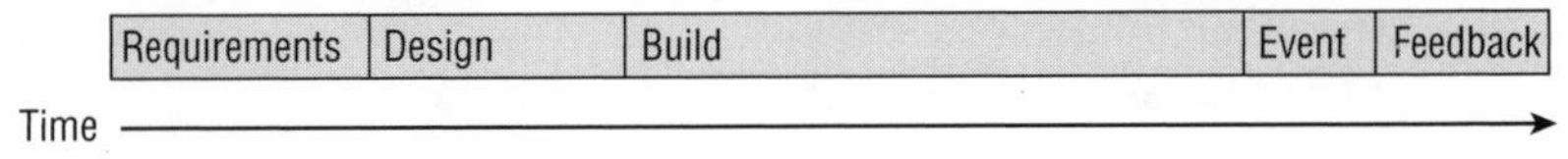

We will be working with Chris as she builds this project using her lifecycle and puts her change management system in place.

In the next chapter, we'll discuss how you build the environment for a successful change management system.

CHAPTER 2

Setting Up for Success

You spent the last chapter reviewing the definitions and fundamentals of change management. From here on, we get down to brass tacks, namely how you successfully set up, manage, and control changes to your project. I start this chapter by talking about the roles and responsibilities that surround change management. I then deal with the elements of a project that get controlled. Next, I cover the timing of change management and how you plan for change. At the conclusion of this chapter, I return you to our case study to see how Chris Baxter applies what you learned in this chapter to the all hands meeting at RemotesUS.

The Roles of Change Management

Let's start with one of the hardest concepts of change management—the roles of the individuals working on a project. You're probably thinking, "How can that be the hardest element?" Well, when you get humans involved in a process and it's not clear what they are supposed to do, it's like trying to herd cats. Everyone's all over the board trying to do what they think is right, but they probably aren't really getting the job done.

NOTE   Don't confuse lots of activities, overtime, and people running around looking busy with real results.

Let's define the roles and responsibilities for each type of person on a typical project—the project manager, the sponsors, the project team, and possibly a new role for you, a change control board.

Project Manager

Project managers have so much to do in a project! At times, it seems as if they have too many things to accomplish to be successful. But if they take the time to plan appropriately and set up processes correctly, their work load lessens and they're able to deliver to the triple constraints I mentioned in Chapter 1—on time, on budget, and to the desired quality.

When it comes to change management, though, let me be specific on what the project manager must do to set up a successful change management system. Let's frame this to-do list in terms of the major skills that a project manager must utilize while working on a project.

Leading In terms of managing a project, the project manager has to demonstrate their leadership abilities. *Leaders* set the context for their team so that the team understands the goals of the project. Leaders make sure that their team members are focused on the project goals. They also work to make sure that roadblocks are removed so the team can execute the project successfully. Leaders motivate and inspire the team to exceed their normal performance ability.

When it comes to change management, leadership skills are also used extensively. Project managers demonstrate their leadership by performing a number of activities. For instance, when you set up the change management system, you need to make sure that the team members understand the purpose of the change management system. You'll want to guarantee that the team members known why the change management system will help deliver the project's objectives. You also need to design and develop your change management system in a way that enables the team to use it properly. You also need to monitor the system to guarantee that the team can successfully use it, and you need to remove any additional roadblocks when they arise. Basically, you must "walk the talk." Utilize the change management system yourself and do not deviate from the process no matter who is asking for or demanding a quick change.

Communicating One of the most important things you learn as a project manager is that you need to communicate, communicate, *communicate*. For your work in the change management process to succeed, you need to exhibit strong communication skill while you perform a variety of activities. For instance, once you've designed and developed the change management system, you need to make sure everybody—the sponsor, the client, the team, and so on—knows how to work with the process. Also, while you are executing the project, you need to continuously communicate why the change management process is necessary. You'll have to educate team members who are new to the process and consistently reinforce how to use the system. In addition, when changes occur on your project, you need to communicate whether a change is approved or denied.

Negotiating Negotiating is one of those activities that just naturally occur when you are working on a project. You'll find that you must negotiate on a regular basis when you implement your change management system. You'll negotiate when you are asked to implement a change that jeopardizes the project's ability to deliver to the triple constraints. And you'll try to negotiate to find a solution that facilitates the change requested while staying within the boundaries of the triple constraints.

Problem Solving *Problem solving* is one of those general management skills that project managers use frequently. You'll often be asked to make a change that jeopardizes your ability to deliver to the triple constrains. You need to work with your team to find a different solution so you can implement the requested change successfully.

Controlling Part of what a project manager must do is *control* the project. You need to guarantee that once the plan is set, it proceeds as planned. Project managers consider control as goal-directed behavior. However, problems may stem from how the team perceives the control exerted by the project manager. For example, they may not see this controlling behavior as positive and may rebel. In addition, you need to influence your team to actively support you so the project can be controlled. You also want to gain your team's positive participation in order to achieve the project's goals. Also, be aware of behaviors that undermine the objectives you've set out. Part of the control involves managing passive-aggressive behavior that has the potential to move the project off track.

Let's now examine the roles and responsibilities that belong to the project's sponsor.

Sponsors

Sponsors need make sure the projects sticks to the vision of what they are trying to achieve with the project they have commissioned. They also determine what projects will help them deliver the organization's strategic goals. They evaluate the progress of the project constantly to see if it completes on time as scheduled. They also monitor the costs of the project to make sure the project stays within the budget.

I've worked with a lot of good project sponsors, but let me tell you about the best of these. In this case, I had just completed planning the project. I knew what the point of the project was and I was able to prove it through my scope statement. (I'll explain scope statements in length later in this chapter.) I had also projected the costs for the entire project to completion. And I had planned my project to the completion date the sponsor had requested. I had my act together. After I walked her through all the data, she simply asked, "How can I support you?" I asked her to remove roadblocks from the team's path when we needed her help doing so. I also covered the following change management points with her:

- Hold the vision. As changes are requested, the sponsor needs to validate that the requested changes are in line with the original intent of the project.

- Toward the end of the project, the project manager reviews the results of the project with the sponsor. If the product does not match the sponsor's vision, she needs to make this clear to the project manager through feedback. The project manager then evaluates what went wrong and possibly initiates a change request to get the product back on track.

- The sponsor heads the change control board. (You'll read more about the board shortly.)

Team Members

Team members are the magic makers who spin straw into gold and create the product. They have a tough job ahead of them, but if the project manager provides clarity and context and makes sure they understand what their contribution needs to be, they will deliver. Here are some of their responsibilities when it comes to change management:

- Avoid making unauthorized changes

  In my project kickoff meeting, I set up team norms for the entire team to follow. There is one norm that's always on my list: Each person needs to agree not to make unauthorized changes to the product of the project. This can sometimes be difficult for a team member to adhere to. Human nature makes people want to please others. When a client asks a developer, "Can you just slip this small change in?" the developer may believe he'll be a hero for helping out. However, it is his responsibility not to do favors for anyone when it comes to changes. The project manager needs to make it clear that the developer is a hero if he follows the team norms.

- Report discrepancies

  Another team norm that I establish is: Report discrepancies. If you find a problem in what you've been asked to create, don't just fix it! This is an important point because again, the team members cannot make unauthorized changes. If they find something wrong, there's a good chance no one else knows about it, and therefore the overall design may be flawed. If your team member fixes it on her own, she may just introduce a new problem because she may use the wrong fix. Also the problem she's discovered may be something that all the other team members need to know about in order to fix their pieces of the product. It's each team member's responsibility to report the problem so the change goes through the change management process.

I'll now cover the last role and set of responsibilities regarding change management—those that apply to the change control board.

Change Control Board

Depending on the size of your project, you might want to establish a *change control board*. Even if you are managing a small- to medium-sized project, you may want to set up this board. You'll want to establish a change control board if all or any of these conditions exist:

- Your project is strategically critical.
- Your project's scope spans several departments.
- Your project is politically sensitive.

Basically this board is implemented to make the hard decisions about whether the project team should accept certain changes.

The change control board should comprise executives or higher-level managers who will be affected by the project. For example, if your project is a new sales compensation system for your sales representatives, you'll want the executive in charge of sales on the board. You'll probably also want the head of Human Resources and the head of Payroll to be board members. Are your sales representatives represented by a union? If so, you'll want the union representative on the board. I think you get the idea. Last but not least, you'll want your project sponsor leading the change control board. Remember, your sponsor holds this project's vision. You want this vision to help govern the changes the board reviews.

What kinds of changes should your board address? Make sure to set some parameters for the types of changes that have to go to the change control board. After all, you don't want all changes reviewed by the board. Not only does this strip the project manager of her authority, it wastes the board's time.

The project manager should have the authority to approve changes that don't have a major impact on the schedule or the budget. Here's a rule of thumb you can use. Have the change control board review and approve any change that

1. Pushes the project over budget.

2. Pushes the project schedule after the committed date.

3. Requires that you rebaseline the project. (I cover baselining in more depth later in the chapter.)

So far, I've covered the roles and responsibilities of each of the players on a project when it comes to change management. Let's now spend some time on what you need to control with a change management process.

What Do We Control?

We control everything! No, I'm really not trying to be a smart aleck, but remember, your job as the project manager is to guarantee that this project delivers to the triple constraints of time, cost, and quality. You need to establish a change management system that is so well managed that no changes happen that jeopardize your goals. Let's get specific and talk about each of the items on which you'll want to focus.

Scope

You need to set up a *scope statement* that defines what is within the project's scope and what isn't. You'll include this scope statement in your change management system. Any time someone wants to make a change, you'll compare that request to the original scope statement so that you can make the right decision. For example, say your scope statement says that the new computer system must run on an existing older server. Then during the system construction phase, the developers ask for a more robust server than the one you originally planned to use. This request would change the scope of the project, so it would need to go through the change management system.

Schedule

You have to establish the schedule for your project. You know exactly what tasks need to be done in what sequence to finish the project to the triple constraints. Here's an example. Let's say your client has been looking at the design of the product and has decided they would like to add a new feature. This new feature will add several additional weeks to the length of the project. This type of request, which impacts the overall length of the project, must go through the change management system.

Budget

The costs of the project have been determined by you during the planning of the project and approved by your sponsor. You know that you'll be able to manage to the exact budget if everything stays on track. But let's say that the sponsor's daughter, who is a highly paid ($150 an hour) media consultant, has just been laid off from her previous position. He has suggested to you that you fill the media consultant position on your project with his daughter. Unfortunately, the position that you have budgeted only allows for a pay rate of $75 an hour. Because this request will impact the budget negatively, it must also go through the change management system.

Contract

Say that you need to procure a specialized resource for your project. You have determined where to get the resource and how much you're willing to pay. Once the contract is set by you and your procurement group, you need to monitor any changes that could potentially affect the contract. For instance, what if your specialized resource, or contractor as they're sometimes called, looks at the design of the product and realizes that they should have set up a time-and-material contract instead of a fixed-price contract. If this happens, they need to come to the project manager and ask to renegotiate the contract based on the additional work they need to do. In other words, this request also needs to go through your change management system.

From these descriptions you can see that many different types of activities need to be funneled through a change management system; you're going to need to keep you eyes open for any change requests and make sure to evaluate all of them. Even a simple request may impact several areas and throw your project off track. At this point, you can also probably sense that you need to apply timing elements to the way this whole process works.

Timing Is Everything

When you are assigned to a project, it's really important to make sure that the work is completed in the right sequence. And I'm not just talking about how the work of the project is performed and sequenced. I'm also talking about how you, the project manager, sequence the project management activities. The sequence should always be

1. Initiate
2. Plan
3. Baseline
4. Execute

If you arrange your project management activities in this order, you've set the basis for a good change management system.

Have you ever been asked to take over an "already in progress" project? If you have, you probably realized fairly quickly that you either had a mess on your hands or a a perfectly planned project in the middle of its execution. When you get an in-flight project, first stop and examine what the previous project manager has accomplished. If they did not finish the planning before they began executing, or if they did not baseline prior to executing, you need to stop the project and go back and finish those steps. Let's examine each of these steps and why this sequence is so important to change management.

Initiating

The *initiating* process is always the first set of activities on a project. It is during this phase that the concepts of the project are usually formalized. Everything discussed in this phase is then expanded upon during the planning phase. Because this phase is all about concepts, you will not employ change management in this phase. You only employ change management once the plan is set.

Planning

Planning is one of the most essential activities on a project, and yet a lot of sponsors and companies believe that this set of activities can be short changed. They think you should just get the project done. Why would you spend so much time talking about what you need to do, when you could just be doing it? If you face this kind of attitude, remember that the software industry has lots of statistics that show it is more cost effective to spend more time designing (planning) than constructing (executing) the system. The cost to correct a defect is much higher the closer you get to delivering the system. Therefore, by spending more time on an effective design, you save time and money in the long run. This also holds true for project planning. The more thought you put into this phase, the better your chances for delivering to the triple constraints of time, cost, and quality.

Make sure you spend the appropriate amount of time on all of the areas of project planning (If you can't remember the knowledge areas, be sure to skim Appendix A.). Most project managers spend most of their time focusing on the project schedule. They tend to think that the most important measure of success is completing the project on time. However, remember that a complete schedule won't help you manage the risks on the project that keep you from delivering on time.

NOTE   Be sure to check out the other books in the Spotlight Series: *Project Manager's Spotlight on Planning,* by Catherine A. Tom-czyk (Sybex, 2005), and *Project Manager's Spotlight on Risk Management,* by Kim Heldman (Sybex, 2005).

While you are creating your project plan, also create your change management process. You'll want to develop and document the process. You also need to communicate the change management process to your project team, client, and sponsor.

Once you've finished planning the complete project, review what you've done with the project team. Also, hold a review session with the sponsor. Do whatever you can to flesh out any missing pieces by engaging the rest of the team in reviews. Go back one more time and add any missing elements. Make sure to document everything you plan to do in one document, the project plan. Now onto the last step of planning—synchronization.

Synchronization

This is one of those steps that I have learned from years of personal experience; you won't find it in other project management textbooks. Remember our discussion about lifecycles in Chapter 1? At the end of the planning process, you need to synchronize the project management lifecycle with the product development lifecycle as shown in Figure 2.1.

FIGURE 2.1: Synchronized lifecycles

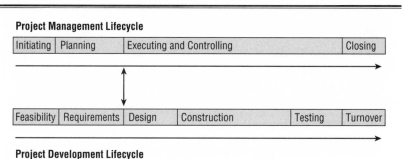

Synchronizing means that you need to align the end of the planning phase with the end of the product requirements phase. The executing and controlling phase of the project management lifecycle needs to coincide exactly with the design and development of the product. You can begin the closing phase of the project at the same time as the turnover phase of the product, but it will run longer.

More importantly, you are now going to synchronize the product requirements with the project plan. But first, you're going to review the project plan one more time. In this review, you need to test the project plan document by asking the following questions:

- Does the project plan reflect the creation of the product of the project? Is every single aspect of the product reflected in the project plan? Have any of the features been left out? Does the project schedule reflect the completion of the product?

- Does the project plan reflect the creation of the product of the project and only the product of the project?

If your answer to any of these questions is no, you either need to change the requirements or change the project plan. If the answer to all of these is yes, you are ready to baseline.

If you want to make this synchronization process easy on yourself, plan for it from the start. Build your project schedule in your mechanized project management software so it reflects each requested product requirement. You can do this by establishing acceptance criteria for the required tasks using the product requirements. Figure 2.2 shows an example project schedule.

In this example, the ABC project has to create a product prototype. The product requirements state that

1. The prototype must be handheld.

2. The prototype must weigh less than 2 pounds.

3. The prototype must be in company colors.

FIGURE 2.2: Requirements as acceptance criteria

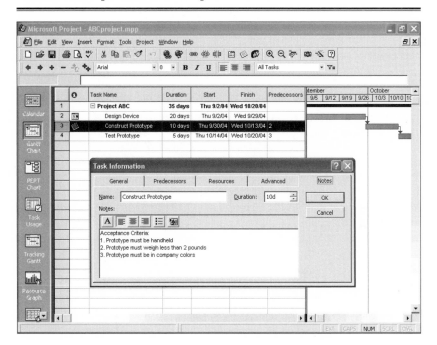

You'll now see these requirements stated as acceptance criteria for the completion of task 3 in the ABC project schedule.

Baselining

Taking a *baseline* just means that you make and keep a copy of what you plan to do so that you can use it for comparative purposes as you execute the project. The philosophy of baselining actually has three components

Components Signatures: You baseline what you plan on doing by reviewing the project plan and the product requirements with the sponsors and the change control board. If they agree with what you have documented, ask them to sign to show their agreement. If they aren't satisfied and won't sign, you need to go back to the planning process and deal with the issues they have brought up.

Copies: You baseline your documents by keeping a copy of the original plan. This way the original is always available so you can compare what you planned on doing with what actually happens. You can keep the original copy either by making sure you establish a version control system for soft copies or by printing out actual hard copies. This is particularly important if you need your project records in dispute situations (mediation, arbitration, litigation, and so on).

Software: You have probably entered your project schedule into a mechanized project management system. Most software packages have a baseline feature. This feature takes and stores a copy of your project schedule for you. The software then provides a mechanized process by which you can compare what you planned to do to what you've done.

Executing

Once your planning is done and the baseline is set, begin executing your project plan. By now you should have also designed your change management system. During execution, you train your team on the process of change management. You monitor the project for unauthorized changes to keep the project on track and to keep it delivering to the triple constraints. We'll get into the process of change management in the next chapter.

Now, let's get back to Chris Baxter now and see how the all hands meeting project is proceeding.

Case Study

Chris Baxter has just finished talking to each of the executives at RemotesUS to find out how they want to handle the requirements gathering for the all hands meeting. Actually, Chris decided to change her strategy after the first meeting with Scott Lanzer. When she asked him what he wanted to do to gather requirements, he had no idea how to proceed. Chris ended up advising him on different techniques for facilitating requirements. The good news is that Scott did assign one of his best employees, Laurie Duggan, to the project as his representative.

Chris then met with the rest of the executives and suggested to each that they have their representatives brainstorm the requirements. Then, after the brainstorming, Chris planned to reengage each of the executives for their input and approval. Each executive provided a resource to work as their representative. The RemotesUS organizational chart with each representative is shown in Figure 2.3.

FIGURE 2.3: RemotesUS org chart with representatives

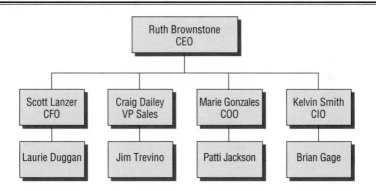

Chris originally looked at this assignment as being beneath her abilities as a project manager. But the more she thinks about it, the more she realizes that this assignment is important to Ruth and the company. She also realizes that she can use this to show Ruth and the executives how talented she really is, which she might be able use to request a promotion. So at this point, Chris has decided to use all of the tools and techniques she has learned previously in her career to make this project shine.

Now that she has come to this decision, Chris decides to call the representatives her core team. She decides it's time to pull them together, create a kickoff meeting, and set up team norms.

It takes about a week before Chris can get everyone together for the kickoff. At this meeting she shares with the team the objectives Ruth established. She isn't allowed to tell them that the company might be closed, but she does make sure that everyone knows dire consequences will materialize if the company does not make major revenue gains with the new product. With that context in place, Chris and her team do some brainstorming and come up with the following team norms:

1. If we miss a project meeting, it's our responsibility to find out what we've missed and if we have any assignments.

2. We will respect each other's opinion.

3. We each agree that we won't make any changes to the agenda for the all hands meeting unless that change is approved through the change management system.

4. If we find a problem with the meeting, we all agree to funnel that problem through the change management system instead of just fixing it on our own.

5. We commit to completing our assignments on time. If we believe we are going to miss an assignment date, we will tell the project manager as soon as we suspect we will miss the date.

With the norms set up, Chris goes back to see Ruth. She has two purposes for this meeting. The first is to provide Ruth with the details of what has transpired until now, and the second is to talk to Ruth about a change control board. Chris explains the concept of the board to Ruth and suggests that the entire executive team act as the board with Ruth as the leader. Ruth agrees to this concept and asks Chris to attend her next staff meeting to brief the rest of the executives on the concept and the process. Chris then updates Ruth on the makeup of her core team and her meetings with the executives.

Chris feels pretty good with what she has accomplished so far, but she knows she needs to get to work on the requirements as well as the project plan and schedule. She decides to rely on her core team to help her build the schedule and gather requirements for the project.

After two weeks of planning and requirements sessions, Chris has a complete list of requirements. Here are some of the requirements the team produced:

- The all hands meeting shall have a motivational sales speaker.

- The all hands meeting shall have break-out time for each executive to meet with his/her staff.
- Ruth will facilitate the opening session of the all hands meeting.
- The all hands meeting will cover the current state of the business.
- The all hands meeting will introduce the new product.
- The all hands meeting will have a new product demo.
- The all hands meeting will be centrally located in the U.S.
- The all hands meeting will have teams work on company process issues.
- The all hands meeting will have two mandatory dinners with guest speakers.
- The all hands meeting will not have spouses accompany the employees to the meeting.
- Each employee will have their own hotel room.
- Liquor will only be served in the evenings.
- The all hands meeting will have an employee rewards and recognition session.
- The all hands meeting will have a feedback questionnaire to be filled in at the end.
- The all hands meeting will have training for each employee on the new product.
- The all hands meeting must be completed before October 31.
- All employees must attend the all hands meeting.

Whew! And that is only the first page of what the team came up with. Chris decides that it is definitely going to be challenging to get all of these items scheduled in three days. She starts thinking that maybe this project is going to be more complex than she originally thought.

Following what she knows to be good project management practices, Chris goes back to the executives and gets their agreement on the requirements. Of course, during these discussions she also picks up 11 new requirements! She then takes the project schedule she has started and completes it, now that she knows the complete requirements.

Chris then tests the project plan and the requirements. She determines that the plan she has formulated will take care of all of the requirements. She also makes sure that no requirements are out of scope for what she has to create.

With the synchronization testing done, Chris is ready for her next meeting with Ruth. At this meeting Chris describes the project schedule and project plan and discusses the requirements. Ruth had lots of questions, but Chris is able to answer them to Ruth's satisfaction. At the end of the session, Ruth signs off on the project and the requirements.

Chris then returns to her desk and baselines the project plan, the schedule, and the requirements. Chris remembers that she has not yet designed her change management system. She realizes she will have to get this done over the weekend because it is already 6 p.m. on Friday night. Chris wonders, where did the week go?

CHAPTER 3

The Process of Change Management

In the last chapter, I spent some time talking about the things you must do to set up a successful change management system. I reviewed the roles of the project manager (PM), the sponsor, and the team members. I also talked about the change control board and when that role is used on projects. Lastly, we discussed timing—when do you plan and when do you baseline? In this discussion of the timing of the change management activities, I also covered the technique of synchronizing the project schedule and the product requirements.

I spend this entire chapter talking about the actual process of change management—what you do on a day-to-day basis to control the project. And of course, at the end of the chapter, you'll see what happening with Chris Baxter and the all hands meeting project at RemotesUS.

Designing Your System

During the planning stage of a project, you actually have to perform several parallel activities: planning the project, gathering the product requirements, and designing the change management system. We covered the first two of these topics in Chapter 2. You have to have this third process ready as soon as you baseline. The way things typically go, you face your first request for change as soon as you finish that baseline.

So what is the process of change management? It is the series of steps you take that guarantee that every change requested is handled properly to the advantage of the project. By *advantage to your project* I am talking about delivering to the triple constraints of time, budget, and desired quality. We'll build this process step by step. Let's get going.

Making a Change to the Project

All of the way through the project execution, you have the opportunity to handle change requests. Did I say opportunity? You may think of these requests as a bother, but they are a natural part of the project's development. When handled well, they either perfect the product vision or reinforce what you were planning all along. Figure 3.1 shows the first step in our change management process.

FIGURE 3.1: Process step 1

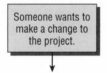

Change requests can come from anyone on your project—team members, clients, sponsors, even the PM. Change requests can also come from people outside of the project, including functional organizations, vendors, and so on.

Change requests usually have to do with a discrepancy in what is planned for the product of the project. Discrepancies can cover specific functions of the product. For example, a requirement states that the product must be able to tolerate hail of 1 inch in diameter. Someone on the project has realized that in Colorado, hail can be anywhere from pea-sized to golf ball–sized. Therefore the requirement needs to change to cover a larger size of hail.

Discrepancies having to do with how the product is created can also occur. For example, say the project schedule shows that task 524, Install House Siding, is a predecessor to task 525, Paint House Siding. If someone on the project realizes that there is a step missing, Apply Primer to House Siding, a discrepancy has occurred.

These disagreements may be valid or invalid. It's the job of the PM, with the help of the team, to determine what changes to accept.

Reviewing the Change Request

Figure 3.2 shows the second step in our change process; this is where the PM rounds up the project team, and together they review the change request.

FIGURE 3.2: Process step 2

During this step, the PM needs to guarantee that every person on the team, or at least each area of the team, is represented during this review. In addition, the PM needs to make sure that the intention of the change request is clear to the team members. The PM should facilitate discussion until all team members' questions are resolved. For large or complex change requests, the PM might consider asking the requestor to attend the review meeting so they can answer team questions.

Determining the Work Required to Make the Change

This process step, depicted in Figure 3.3, requires the team members to return to their work area to do some analysis.

FIGURE 3.3: Process step 3

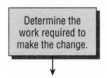

At this time, their job is to determine what it will take to implement the change request. They determine the impact by examining what they are creating for the project as well as how they plan to create the product. Once this analysis is complete, they need to determine the following:

- The duration needed to make the change request

- The work effort needed to make the change request

- The resources needed to make the change request

- The steps required to make the change request, including dependencies with other areas of the project

- The potential risks to the project that might result from making this change

They then provide the PM with all this documentation.

Accumulating the Required Work

The step depicted in Figure 3.4 requires work from the PM.

FIGURE 3.4: Process step 4

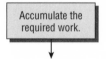

The PM takes all of the information provided by the team members and builds a complete picture of what it will take to make the requested change. Once the PM has accumulated everything, they know

- The total time it will take to complete the change

- The total amount of effort they will need to complete the change, which will determine the cost of the change

- All of the resources required to complete the change

- The risks associated with making the change

The one thing they still need to determine is the sequence of the steps they need to take to complete the change. To determine this, the PM analyzes all of the steps and dependencies noted by the team members. They then lay out the proper sequence of the tasks that need to be done. Of course, they take into account all of the dependencies described by the team members. Basically, the PM creates a mini project schedule for just this change, as shown in Figure 3.5.

FIGURE 3.5: Mini schedule of the change request

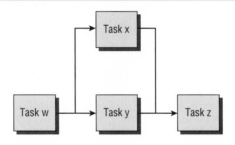

Determining the Impact to the Project Plan and Requirements

Step 5, depicted in Figure 3.6, is the tough part of the change management process.

FIGURE 3.6: Process step 5

The PM must perform two separate examinations in this step: analyzing the impact to the project plan and analyzing the impact to the requirements. The change request could impact one or both of these elements. I analyze both here because they are exactly in sync; the project plan reflects only what this project is creating. If you make a change to one, you need to resynchronize both.

Let's start this analysis with the *project schedule*, one of the components of the project plan. First take the project schedule and make a copy of it for this "what if" scenario, as shown in Figure 3.7. Because you don't yet know whether this change will be approved or denied, you don't want to make changes to your real work plan.

FIGURE 3.7: Copy of the project schedule

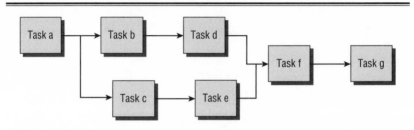

Okay, now take that mini schedule shown in Figure 3.5 and determine exactly where it should be inserted into the existing project schedule (Figure 3.7). Make sure that the start of the mini schedule has tasks that precede it from the original plan. Also make sure that the end of the mini schedule has successor tasks in the original schedule. When you're through, you're "what if" project schedule should look like Figure 3.8.

Now you need to perform your regular project management magic and calculate the new critical path for the "what if" project schedule. (If you don't remember how to calculate the critical path, see Appendix C.) With the new critical path, you can tell what the end date is for the project. Ask yourself, "Is the end date the same as the original plan?" If it isn't, you need to see if *crashing* or *fast tracking* the project moves the end back to the original date.

Now let's examine the costs of the project, another component of the project plan. You should have received work effort estimates from each of your team members. You need to add the estimates together to determine the total cost of the change request. Ask yourself, "Can this cost be absorbed into the cost of the project without going over budget?" Now ask yourself, "Do I have the resources necessary to complete the change?" Along with the work effort estimates, your team should also provide you with the resources you need to complete the change.

FIGURE 3.8: "What if" project schedule

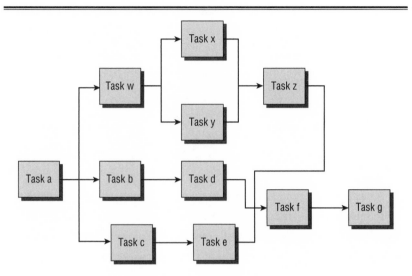

Next, review the quality guidelines, which make up another component of the project plan. Compare what you have been asked to change to the quality guidelines. Ask yourself, "Will this change request prevent us from achieving these quality guidelines?"

Okay, you've completed the first of two examinations that must be done at this step; now get ready to complete the second. This examination requires you to analyze the change request against the product requirements. Ask yourself, "Does this change request invalidate any of the requirements for this product?" If it does, you need to take the renegotiation of that requirement into consideration as part of your decision process.

Having an Impact on the Triple Constraints

You've gathered a lot of data through the change management process. It's now time to analyze it all and determine the impact it has on the triple constraints of time, budget, and defined quality, as shown in the decision step in Figure 3.9.

FIGURE 3.9: Process step 6

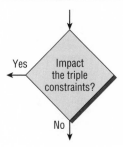

After asking yourself the questions from the preceding step, you know if the schedule, the budget, the defined quality, and the requirements are impacted negatively by the change request. If none of them are affected, you can probably decide to accept the change request. I say *probably* here because, even though it looks like this change can be easily absorbed, it still creates some additional risk that needs to be analyzed. We'll talk more about that in Chapter 5.

If even one of the triple constraints is affected by the change request, you need to get approval from your change control board (if you have one). If you don't have a change control board, you need to get your sponsor to concur before you agree to approve the change.

With this last decision step, you complete the design of your change management process. Figure 3.10 shows how the entire process flows.

A Few More "To Dos"

You may think that you are finished designing your change process at this point. In reality, you still have a few more things to do.

First, you need to set up a recurring meeting in which you discuss change control activities. You can combine this meeting with your regular status meetings at whatever frequency you prefer. Here is a rule of thumb for the frequency of your status meetings: How long can a task be out of control without your knowledge? For example, you have a task that is one

FIGURE 3.10: Change management process

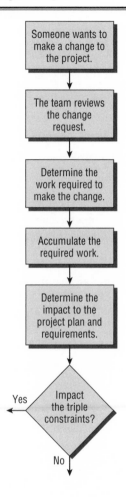

month in length and starts on June 15. You decide to have your status meeting once a month on the last day of the month. On June 30 you have your status meeting and everyone reports that their tasks are on time. No task is projected to complete later than expected. On July 5 the person working on the month-long task starts running into trouble. They realize they are falling behind but believe they can catch up before the task is due.

July 15 comes and goes and the task is not done. Because you have a status meeting on July 31, you will not know the task is incomplete until then. Can you afford to allow that task to slip two weeks and not know about it? How soon do you need to know that a task is slipping?

The answer to this question sets your frequency. Most PMs choose to have such a meeting every week, or every other week, depending on the length as well as the stage of the project.

Now let's get back to your change control meeting. Most PMs choose to start having their change control meetings once every two weeks at the beginning of the execution phase. Soon you will be able to tell whether this frequency will work from the number of requests you receive. If you have lots of requests, you need to meet every week or even more often. If you have very few requests, every other week may work, or you may want to meet only when you get a request.

Second, you need to remember that most change requests that you work on need to be expedited through the process. You will want to set up deadlines for each of the steps of your change management process. Make sure that the entire team understands the due dates for each of these change management activities.

And lastly, remember that 80 percent of a PM's job is communication? Well here is another instance where that skill comes into play.

You now need to conduct a review meeting with all of the team members to explain how the change management process is going to work. In this meeting, walk through the process step by step, answering questions and making sure that each team member understands the process. At this point, you also reiterate the team norm of no unauthorized changes.

You also need to brief the other players on the project on the change management process. You'll want to include your sponsor and especially the clients; they need to know that they have to abide by the process if they want anything changed.

Now let's see what Chris Baxter has done with the change management process at RemotesUS.

Case Study

Over the weekend, Chris Baxter begins designing her change management process for the RemotesUS all hands meeting project. Even before the weekend, she was thinking that putting these types of processes into an all hands meeting is overkill, but she decides to put a process in place just in case. She really wants to shine on this project and thinks this process will show Ruth that she knows what she's doing.

Chris isn't able to finish the design of the change management system over the weekend because she feels she needs some input from her core team. She wants to make sure that the core team has time to do the review and analysis the process requires and is afraid that they won't have time with their busy schedules.

On Monday, Chris meets with the core team and, just as she suspected, two of the core team are very worried about having the time to work the change management process. Chris decides that their participation is very important to the overall project's success, so she decides to escalate. Chris sets up meetings with Kelvin Smith the CIO and Craig Dailey the VP of Sales. Chris thinks that, with a little coaxing, she can get both of them to commit their resources fully to the project team.

The meeting with Kelvin goes well. He agrees that Brian needs to participate in all of the team activities, including the change management activities. The only problem with this commitment is that he says Brian will have to "suck up" the additional time. Kelvin is not able to reduce his workload.

The meeting with Craig is not as successful. Craig heads up sales, and when Jim Trevino is busy with this administrative work, he's not making sales. At this time, with the new product coming online, Craig doesn't think he can spare any additional time for Jim. In fact, Craig regrets putting Jim on the team in the first place. Chris and Craig negotiate for about an hour before they agree that another of Craig's employees, Jennifer Peters, will replace Jim altogether. Jennifer is a newer salesperson and is not as critical as Jim. Figure 3.11 show the replacement person on the organizational chart.

FIGURE 3.11: New organizational chart

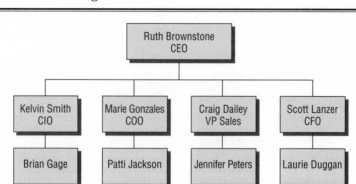

Chris isn't thrilled with this change because it means she has to get Jennifer up to speed on everything that the team has already accomplished, but at least she now has a full-time person representing Craig's interests in the all hands meeting.

Chris spends the next two days in meetings with Jennifer updating her on all of the specifics of the project. First Chris discusses the requirements with her. Next, she covers all of the aspects of the project plan. Finally, Chris pulls the entire team together and they review the team norms. Chris wants to give Jennifer a chance to add any norms that are important to her. She also wants Jennifer to concur on the team norms in front of the other team members.

With Jennifer up to speed, Chris goes back to completing the design of the change management process. When she is through, it looks like the diagram in Figure 3.12.

Chris then sits down with the core team and reviews the change process. They think it is okay and say they can abide by the process. However, each expresses worry about how much time this may take. Chris and the team decide to only hold a change control meeting when a request needs to be reviewed. They all think that they have done a wonderful job on the project plan and requirements and that they will need to make very few changes.

FIGURE 3.12: Chris' change control process

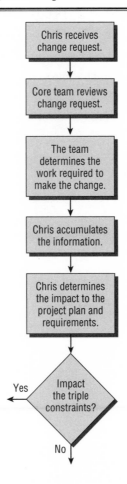

On Friday, Chris tries to get on both Ruth's and the executives' calendars to brief them on the change control process. She is disappointed when she finds out that she will not get to attend Ruth's staff meeting until next Tuesday. She and the team had been planning to design the agenda for the all hands meeting on Monday. That design work would officially kick off the execution phase of the project. She figures she'll probably be okay if the final approval is one day later than she planned. What could a day hurt?

When Chris gets back to her desk late on Friday afternoon, she discovers a voice-mail message from Craig Dailey. Craig says, "I know I signed your requirements document, but I've really been thinking about this meeting. You need to set aside some time for my group to go through a professional sales training class. You should be able to find something pretty cheap that will only last a day or so. Of course I want to approve what you come up with. Let me know what you find."

And so it begins....

CHAPTER 4

The Output of Change Management

In the last chapter, you learned how to design the change management system you will use throughout project execution. Step by step, we discussed what you do on a day-to-day basis for every change that comes your way. In this chapter, I talk about the output of that process—what exactly do you do with a change request after you've determined if you're going to approve or deny it? Here, I get into the dynamics of change management and what happens to your project plan when a large change request is approved. I also spend some time covering what to do when people bypass the system.

At the end of the chapter, we check in on Chris Baxter to find out how she handled that last minute request and other change requests for the all hands meeting.

Now What?

So far, you've learned how to create a change management process that shows what needs to be done to monitor and control changes. Now that you're nearing the end of the process and understand the impact to the triple constraints, you might ask yourself, "What do I do now?" With that question in mind, let's talk about the output of the change management process. The output of our process is as follows:

- If the change *is denied,* notify the team and the requestor.
- If the change *is approved and affects the triple constraints,* rebaseline the project and notify the team and the requestor.

- If the change *is approved regardless of the impacts to the triple constraints,* update and resynchronize the project plan and the requirements and notify the team and the requestor.

In the previous chapter, I showed this last step of the change management system, depicted in Figure 4.1, as a decision point. At this point, we asked ourselves, "Are the triple constraints impacted by the change request?" Depending on the answer, we now take different actions.

FIGURE 4.1: The change management process

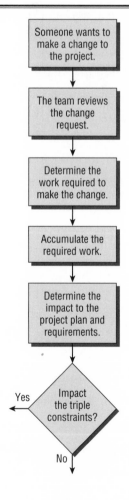

Yes, the Triple Constraints Are Impacted

If your answer to the decision point is yes, you need to take output step 1, depicted in Figure 4.2—take the change request to your change control board. (In Chapter 2, I talked briefly about this board and who should participate on it.) If the answer is no, jump ahead to output step 5, discussed later in this chapter.

FIGURE 4.2: Output step 1

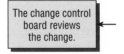

This decision on impacting the triple constraints is based on the fact that this change request is so big, it is going to take the project off course. By implementing this change, the schedule may become longer, or the costs may exceed their current budget, or the quality of the project's product may be compromised.

Most project managers do not have the authority to make such a major decision. If this is the case in your situation, take the change request to the change control board for approval. If you aren't using a change control board on your project, you need to get the change approved by your executive sponsor. Regardless of whether you're getting approval from the change control board or your sponsor, you should perform the same activities.

You'll want to convene the board for a meeting on a specific date and time to get their decision on the change request. This is going to be a very important meeting, and you'll want to prepare accordingly. Make sure that you

- Provide an agenda beforehand so that everyone knows what changes are going to be discussed.

- Document a complete overview of the request so that each participant understands it.

- Document the complete impacts on the project. How much additional time will you need? How much additional money will be required? What changes will be made to the product of the project? Also make sure to document any assumptions associated with both an approval as well as a rejection.

- Are ready to provide clear and concise information on which of the triple constraints will be missed if this change is approved.

- Have thought about "what if" alternatives that might be employed instead of the change request if any are available.

Because the outcome of your project depends on the decision the change control board makes, you don't want to take any chances. You know that most of the time, major decisions are already made before the meeting starts. You also already know whether or not this change is the right thing to do for your project. For instance, perhaps this change request is nothing more than the vendetta of a disgruntled employee who doesn't want to see the project replace their job. Or perhaps the change is politically motivated by an employee who is seeking more power. Regardless of the motivation behind the change, you know whether it will help you deliver the right project for your company.

With all this in mind, take the time to meet with key members of the change control board before the actual meeting. Explain your reasoning for approving or denying the change to them. Explain the politics behind the change if there are any. Give them enough ammunition to help them make the right decision—the decision that is the right one for the project. Basically, get the decisions made before you even get into the change control board meeting.

NOTE   Don't wait for important decisions to be made at a formal meeting. Update decision makers ahead of time on the pros and cons of the decision outcome. Know where the decision makers stand before the meeting starts.

Did you establish ground rules for your change control board? If you didn't when you established the board, it's a good idea to get these set up at the beginning of the first meeting. One of the things you'll want to determine is how they will make their decisions. Does the majority rule? Does the decision have to be unanimous? Does the executive sponsor have an overruling vote? Make sure you establish these parameters *before* the board makes its first decision or you may end up with a situation like a hung jury, with no decision made and your project in limbo.

Okay, it's now time for the change control board meeting. Your executive sponsor will run the meeting, but you will provide the information. If you've done your homework properly, the meeting should be fairly quick. The board should analyze the request and provide a decision before the meeting is over. Figure 4.3 shows the decision step the change control board is making.

FIGURE 4.3: Output step 2

The Board Denies the Change

If the board denies the change request, your job is easy. You perform two official tasks, as depicted in Figure 4.4:

1. Notify the requestor that the change request has been denied.

2. Notify the project team that the change request has been denied.

FIGURE 4.4: Output step 3

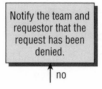

This official decision needs to be officially documented. In Chapter 6, I'll tell you about the forms to use for this documentation, but for now, just know that you need to make sure that everyone on your team gets information about and understands the outcome of the decision. Do whatever you have to do to make sure the decision is understood—post the decision to the project website, send an email notification to every project participant, read the form to everyone at a team meeting, and so on. You don't want any denied changes getting implemented because a team member didn't get the word.

Unofficially, you want to see if your team has lost focus because of the change request. Sometimes a request is very big and disrupting to the team. People sometimes lose focus on the objectives of the project because their attention has been diverted by the change request. If the team has lost focus because of the change request, get the team back together for a team meeting and walk them through the objectives of the project again. Get them refocused and hopefully back to the pace of development at which they were working prior to the disruption of the change request.

The Board Approves the Change

If the change control board approves the change request, you'll have a couple of things to accomplish. (This output step is depicted in Figure 4.5.) First, you have to rebaseline. Remember, the reason you brought this change request to the change control board in the first place is because it is so big that it changes one of more of the triple constraints.

FIGURE 4.5: Output step 4

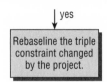

To rebaseline, go back to your original analysis and determine which one (or all) of the triple constraints is modified by this change request.

- If the schedule will be changed, rebaseline the project schedule.
- If the budget will be changed, rebaseline the budget for the project.
- If the quality will be impacted, you may need to rebaseline scope or requirement documents.

Did you notice we said "or all" in the previous paragraph? The change being approved may change all of your triple constraints or may impact only two, or just one. Be sure to rebaseline accordingly.

You may be wondering about the activity of rebaselining. In Chapter 2, I talked about the original baseline of the project and said that taking a baseline is as simple as keeping a copy of what you plan to do for comparative purposes as you execute the project. You do exactly the same thing here. This change is so big you need to take another snapshot of your project after the change has been applied for comparative purposes as you continue executing your project. At this point, you may also want to get new signatures on your project plan, requirements, and other important documents.

You've probably been thinking about the hassle of dealing with this huge change request and what problems it causes. Another way to look at this impact is to assume all bets are off. Everything you have planned to do up to this point has changed. You now have a new plan. If your project was starting to get off course before you received the change request, you now have the chance to reset the expectations for the project and get it back on track. Remember, make sure that all of your planning for change requests is very comprehensive. You may have to live with the outcome of that plan.

Once you've completed the rebaseline, you have other duties to attend to, but first let's cover what happens if the change request won't impact the triple constraints.

The Triple Constraints Are Not Impacted

Remember the first decision we had made at the end of our change request process, depicted back in Figure 4.1? Whether the triple constraints were impacted or not?

So far, I have talked all about the scenario for a large change request that impacts the triple constraints. Now let's talk about the type of change that doesn't affect these constraints. This type of change is small enough that you don't have to get the change control board involved. You, the project manager, can make the decision on this type of change by yourself. The reason that the change doesn't impact the triple constraints is that it can be handled with *slack time* or a *contingency budget* that you build into your project. Let's take a second to talk about each of these points.

Slack/float time When you originally planned your project, you sequenced your project schedule's tasks in the exact order in which you thought they should be performed. With that accomplished, you calculated the *critical path*. (Refer to Appendix C for a discussion on critical path and what paths have slack or float.) The critical path contains no slack time; this means that if any task slips, the end date of your project is delayed. There are many paths through your network diagram and usually only one is a critical path. If a change request is able to fit into a set of non-critical path activities and uses some of the slack time, you won't delay the project.

Contingency budget or management reserve The same philosophy of slack or float also holds true for your budget. You may be one of the lucky project managers who is able to have a little extra money put away for your project that you can use for these types of situations. Most of us, however, don't have the luxury of having these types of funds available. This extra funding is called a contingency budget or a *managerial reserve*.

You also may run into situations in the project that require less money than you originally planned. Perhaps you rented a backhoe at a lower rate than you expected. If that is the case, you have a situation in which you have a little extra budget available that can cover the change request.

Okay now that you know whether you have additional time or funding, it's time for you to make the decision on whether to approve or deny the change request, as shown in Figure 4.6.

FIGURE 4.6: Output step 5

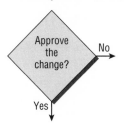

You now need to weigh the pros and cons of the change request the same way you ask the change control board to do. You need to ask yourself these types of questions:

- Will this change improve the product of the project?

- Will this change improve the way the project is organized or executed?

You also may encounter political reasons for approving the change. Ask yourself these types of questions:

- Who initiated the change request? Will this person jeopardize the project if I deny this change?

- Will the approval or denial of this change create an adversarial climate for the project team?

- Will approving this change make the sponsor happy?

You get the picture.

NOTE   Here' some advice from someone who has been in your shoes before. Deny as many change requests as you can. Each change request you and your team have to review causes a little more disruption and takes a little more of your precious project time. I'll talk at length about this subject in the next chapter.

Okay, you've weighed the pros and cons and you are ready to make your decision.

The Project Manager Denies the Change Request

If you decide to deny the change request, perform the following steps, which are outlined in Figure 4.7.

1. Notify the requestor.

2. Notify the project team.

FIGURE 4.7: Output step 6

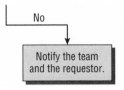

Once again, you're going to want to check out the team and see where their heads are. Have they lost focus on the objectives of the project? If the team has lost focus because of the change request, get them back together for a team meeting and walk them through the original project objectives.

Get them refocused and hopefully back to the development pace at which they were working prior to the disruption of the change request.

The Project Manager Approves the Change Request

After due diligence, you've decided to approve the change request. It's the right thing for the project regardless of whether it's really needed or whether there are political reasons for approving it.

When you give this approval, you will have four activities to perform. Figure 4.8 shows the first two activities.

FIGURE 4.8: Output step 7

First you need to update the project schedule. Remember the mini schedule and "what if" project schedule you created back in process step 5 in the last chapter? Now take that mini schedule and insert it into your real schedule. That "what if" schedule is now the one you will continue executing.

Be sure to update the project costs with the new cost of the change request. Also, review your other project documents and update them as needed.

The next activity in output step 7 is resynchronizing the project plan with the requirements. Initially, you performed a synchronization of the project plan and the product requirements when you complete the project planning and the product requirements. Every time you approve a change request, you need to resynchronize. You always want your project plan to reflect exactly what you are creating and nothing more. If anything else is in the project plan, then your project is out of scope.

Now you conduct a review of the project plan. In this review, you test the project plan document by asking the following questions:

- Does the project plan reflect the creation of the product of the project? Is every single aspect of the product reflected in the project plan? Have any of the features been left out? Does the project schedule reflect the completion of the product? Is the change request now reflected in the project plan?

- Does the project plan reflect the creation of the product of the project and only the product of the project? Have the requirements been updated to reflect the new change request?

Depending on the answers to these questions, you may need to conduct more updates until the project plan exactly reflects the requirements of the project's product. When you finish this synchronization, you are ready to continue your updating activities.

Figure 4.7 (shown earlier) also depicts the last set of activities that you must perform when you approve a change request—you still notify the requestor and the project team on the final decision regarding the change.

First, you notify the requestor that their change request has been approved. Make sure when you do so that you thank this person for following the process. Then, you also notify the team that the change request has been approved. How you handle this notification is important. It's probably best to have a meeting with the project team and

- Explain to them why the change request was approved.

- Show them exactly where the change request fits into the existing project schedule.

- Show them exactly where the change request modified the product requirements.

- Show them how the change management process works to benefit the project.

Once again you need to work with the team to get them back on track. Remember, change requests can be disrupting just because they move the focus away from the work the team is performing.

This entire series of activities you have performed to complete the change request process is the same set of activities that you perform when the board approves a change request. The only difference is that when the board approves a change request, you need to rebaseline because you've impacted one or more of the triple constraints.

Process Review

You have now completed the entire process for your change management system, as depicted in Figure 4.9.

You'll probably design your process for your project in a very similar manner. Here are some keys to your design:

- The team gets to look at everything that will impact their work. This allows them to have a voice in what is happening and builds buy-in from the team.

- Each change request has adequate planning. You never know what will be approved or denied, so you plan each change request extensively. If you don't, you may have to live with a change that you barely looked at.

- Get approval at the appropriate level. If the triple constraints are impacted, you need approval from a higher authority than the project manager.

- Communicate, communicate, communicate. Make sure everyone involved knows the status and the final decision regarding each change request.

- Keep the team focused on the objectives of the project even as they change.

As we discuss next, your change management process design needs to fit into your product development and project management lifecycles.

FIGURE 4.9: Change management process

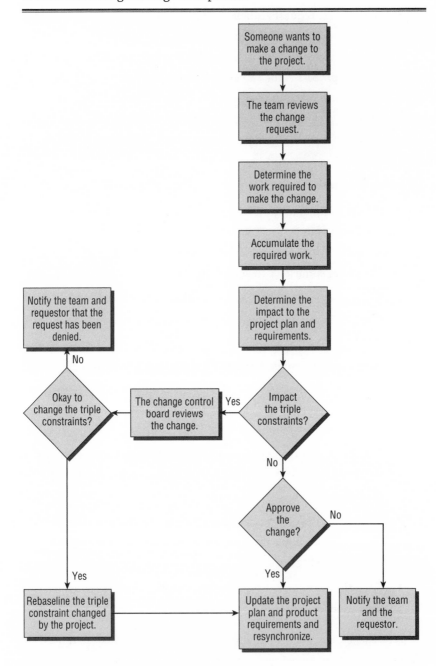

The Process within the Lifecycles

Remember that in your change process, as in the setup of your change management system, timing is everything. You normally manage change during the executing and controlling processes of a project management lifecycle. You may not be using this change management process until then, but it behooves you to deal with change as early in the lifecycle as possible.

Problems you find early in the lifecycle are faster to deal with and cheaper to fix. Think about the impact your change may have on the project depending upon where you are in the lifecycle. Usually you won't find any problems or changes in the initiating phase; this is because the ideas for the project are just being formulated at that stage. If you find problems in the planning phase, you should incorporate the solutions into what you plan to create. If you find problems are during the executing and controlling phases, you must make sure they are analyzed through the change management system before you incorporate them into the plan. Of course, problems you do not find until late in the lifecycle can be disastrous for the completion of the project. And, needless to say, problems you don't find at all during the project may have an even worse effect in the customer's hands.

Whenever you find a problem, you need to replan as I described earlier in this chapter. You need to bring discrepancies you find in later phases back to the planning phase to determine the impact they will have on the requirements and the project plan (this is depicted in Figure 4.10). Once you have replanned and approved those discrepancies, you need to resynchronize the project plan and requirements.

FIGURE 4.10: Change management within the lifecycles

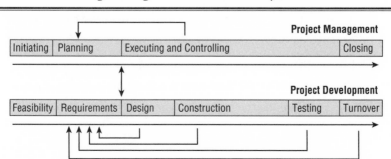

The whole idea here is to get the right project completed for the company. You manage change for the good of your project.

Exceptions

Let's say you have a well-meaning developer working on your project. He has a great working relationship with the client. So good, in fact, that whenever the client wants a feature change, she goes directly to the developer and he sneaks the changes in so she doesn't have to do any of that change management paperwork. Needless to say, the developer keeps slipping the completion of his tasks and is starting to run the project behind schedule.

You're going to run into all sorts of exceptions to the change management process. You will come across situations in which people are subverting the system because they don't want to deal with it, where people believe they don't have to play by the rules, and where people's good intentions just get in the way.

So what's wrong with a little exception processing? A lot! If this developer puts in a new product feature, you may have the following types of problems with the remainder of the project:

- No one else on the project realizes that this feature has been included. As the product goes through testing, no one knows to test this feature and as a result, it may not work when it gets into the hands of the customer.

- The new feature takes more time than the developer thought. The length of the project is extended because the developer keeps missing his dates, thus impacting the triple constraints.

- The product documentation and training doesn't match the product features.

- When others get wind of someone not following the process, they wonder why they are bothering to follow it, and they probably start making their own changes outside of the process.

Basically chaos could reign if you don't get these people back into the process. Okay, it might not be that bad, but you could have a mess on your hands. So what do you do to keep people in the process and get them back in when they deviate from the process?

You set up a team norm that says that no one can make unauthorized changes to the project. This means that everyone should be on track with staying in the process. You then monitor this team norm at every team meeting, asking them whether the process is being followed. If you continually focus on this team norm, people know that you are serious about it.

The first time you find an unauthorized change, regardless of whether it has just been started or is completely finished, you must stop it. You have to stop this behavior immediately and make sure that the team and the requestor know it will not be tolerated. First, you'll want to pull the perpetrator aside and make sure they understand that they have violated the team norms. Let them know that this won't be tolerated and that future problems may lead to their removal from the team. Then have them go back and remove the unauthorized change from the product. At the next team meeting, focus again on the team norms making sure that everyone understands that deviating from the process won't be tolerated and that there are consequences for not following the team norms. Remember, you have to show the team that you are serious or no one will follow the process. Also, the first time a change is done correctly, be sure to point this out to the entire team and publicly acknowledge whoever worked the process correctly. This small acknowledgement strengthens the process in the entire team's mind.

Escalations

So you've just finished taking a change request through the entire process. You've decided to reject a change request that you've decided can wait for the next release of the product. After you've notified the entire team, a couple of team members come to you and tell you that they disagree with your decision. The last thing you want is disgruntled team members. How do you handle these types of situations?

A nice tool for a project manager to use for just these types of situations is an *escalation process*. This process lines out exactly how decisions are made at every level of the project organization. You can use this process to help deal with any type of escalation regardless of whether or not it originates with change requests. A simple escalation process is depicted in Figure 4.11.

FIGURE 4.11: Escalation process

This diagram shows how escalations should be handled in an organization in which a project manager reports to a program manager. Decisions should always be made by the most appropriate and lowest level of the project. In this example, we show that the responsible task owner can make some decisions. If an escalation occurs at that level, the decision then goes to the core team leader. If the core team leader can't handle the situation, the decision goes to the project manager. Hopefully most of your escalations can be solved with these few people.

On some rare occasions, you will encounter escalations the project manager can't settle. If that is the case, according to our diagram in Figure 4.11, the next level up is the program director. Notice that the program director and the change control board are on the same level. Internal disputes go to the program director; change control disputes go to the change control board. Disputes the change control board or the program director can't settle are finally sent to the executive sponsor. The executive sponsor is usually the one whose neck and money are on the line for this project.

Once you've determined what your escalation process should be, you need to document it. Make sure you communicate the process to everyone on your team. Also, be sure to post the process where people will be able to see it. Use this process whenever escalations occur on your project.

Now let's head back to the all hands meeting project and see how Chris Baxter's change management system is working.

Case Study

Chris frets about the phone message from Craig Dailey most of the weekend. She is shocked that her first change request has happened before she has even had time to brief Ruth and the executives on what the process is going to be. Chris feels that the professional sales training that Craig requested is really out of scope for the all hands meeting. However, she also understands why he thinks it is important. Over the weekend, she decides to handle Craig's request as the first official change request. But this reminds her that she needs to hurry up and get the process communicated to the executives.

On Monday, Chris and the core team create a draft agenda for the all hands meeting. They design the meeting based on the requirements they gathered earlier in the project. Chris and the team think that the agenda looks pretty good and are pleased that they seem to be keeping the meeting within the parameters Ruth requires. The draft agenda is for three business days in October, a Wednesday through Friday, and the total anticipated cost is $45,000. However, this design does not include Craig's request.

Chris also calls Craig on Monday to let him know she is investigating his request. She begins some preliminary investigations to find out what it takes to put on a professional sales training class. As Chris begins her analysis, she realizes that in the change process she defined, she did not take care of the way the final decision of a change request is handled. She decides to modify her process. Figure 4.12 shows Chris' updated process.

FIGURE 4.12: Chris' updated change management process

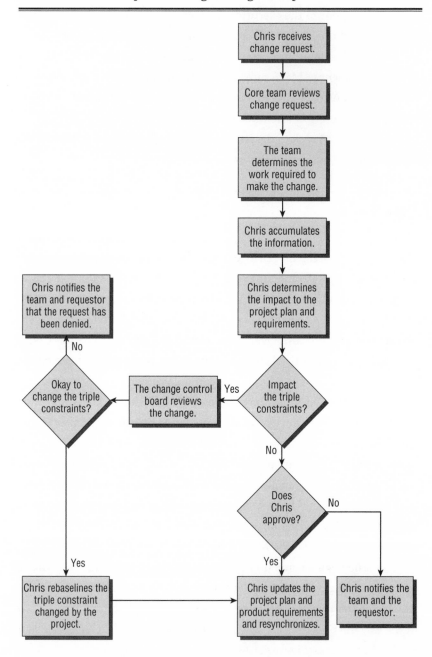

On Tuesday, Chris attends Ruth's staff meeting. She walks the executives through the updated change request process. After she receives their agreement on the process, she asks to talk to Craig privately about his request.

Craig isn't pleased that his request has to go through this new process. He feels that the sales training should have been worked into the original plan. Chris explains that if she worked his request into the original plan, the design of the agenda would have been delayed. That delay, in turn, would create delays for airfare bookings and hotel arrangements. She explains that because she did not want to jeopardize the whole plan as a result of this request, she decided to handle it as the first change order. Craig understands but is pretty adamant that this request gets approved quickly. Chris assures him that the core team will get working on it immediately.

Chris is actually pretty worried about this change request. She knows she only has $5,000 to spend and a few slack hours left in the agenda—probably not enough to cover this type of training.

Later on Tuesday afternoon, Chris gets the core team together to talk about the change request. She informs them of the details of what Craig is requesting. They promise to analyze the additional work and get back to Chris on Thursday on what it will take to put on the sales training. Chris is worried that it is going to take so long to finish the analysis, but she knows that these folks are also trying to do their normal jobs in addition to working on firming up the agenda for the all hands meeting. They are doing things like booking speakers, pricing hotels, checking airfares, and so on.

Tuesday night Chris has a hard time getting to sleep because she is still trying to figure out how she can accommodate Craig and still stay within the parameters Ruth provided. Chris really feels that the sales training is out of scope for an all hands meeting. However, she also knows that the fate of the company rides on the sales from this new product. Before finally falling into a fitful sleep, she decides to try to find some alternatives to what Craig has requested. Chris spends Wednesday looking for alternatives.

Thursday morning, Chris meets with the core team and gathers all the information they provide. She finds out that there is a sales training class that can be done in eight hours for $2500. The kicker, though, is that the agenda can't accommodate an additional eight hours. She knows she can't have the sales training concurrent to the all hands meeting because the sales team needs to be part of the regular agenda. And if she has the sales team come to the all hands meeting a day early, she goes over the three business days Ruth requires. Besides, in addition to the $2500 for the training, she would need to put the sales people up for an additional night, which would definitely cost more. Can she keep the hotel costs for the extra night under $2500? And even if she can, that leaves her with no budget contingency. It really looks like the change can't be approved.

Chris knows that the triple constraints will be impacted by this change, and so she has to meet with the change control board to get this approved. Chris sets up the change control board meeting for the next Tuesday.

On Friday, Chris continues to look for a workaround. She knows the sales training is a good idea. After all, the sales team needs the training and the sales team will all be in the same city at the same time. So, though the sales training isn't good for the all hands meeting project, it is good for the company. Also, Craig is very influential. Keeping him happy might be key to a future promotion for Chris. Chris decides to keep working on a solution over the weekend.

Monday morning Chris goes to Craig Dailey's office even before she visits her own desk. She had a brainstorm over the weekend and wants to propose some ideas to Craig. She explains the constraints around the all hands meeting to Craig. She also tells him how important she knows this training is. She suggests to Craig that they keep the sales team over Friday and Saturday night and fly them home Sunday morning. In this scenario, the training would be conducted on Saturday (she had already contacted the training vendor and knows this is an option). This brainstorm actually reduces the overall budget for the all hands meeting to $42,500 because the Saturday night stay reduces the plane fare for the sales team. However, she does need an additional $2000 for the Friday and Saturday hotel nights, which brings her budget back up to $44,500. She suggests that Craig pay the $2500 training fee out of his departmental budget, so she will still have a little contingency reserve in case she has other emergencies. Craig finally agrees when he hears that the probable site of the all hands meeting is going to be Las Vegas. He knows his team won't mind staying over in Las Vegas.

Chris goes back to her desk and cancels the change control board meeting for Tuesday because the triple constraints are not going to be impacted after all. She updates her project documents and resynchronizes her plan and the new requirements. She then lets her core team know that the change request has been modified and approved. One down, how many more to go?

Just as she's getting settled, Chris notices a revised agenda on her desk. While she was busy with Craig's request, her team kept their heads down and continued their work. She notices that two of the slack hours have been replaced with a facilitated team building session at a cost of $4000. "Here we go again!" she thinks.

CHAPTER 5

The Incremental Effect

In the last chapter, you worked on the design of your change management system. You spent time working on the output of your system—exactly what you should do when you have enough information to decide whether you should or shouldn't accept the change. I also spent some time talking about what happens when people work outside of the process.

In this chapter, I talk about the incremental effect—what happens when a lot of changes come your way during the execution of your project. I also add some more steps to your change management process. At the end of the chapter, we return to Chris Baxter and find out how she decides to handle that unauthorized addition to the all hands meeting agenda. You also see what other changes are coming her way and how she handles them. Let's start this chapter with a story from my past experience.

I once worked on a project that was very big. It had a total duration of 9 months and a budget of approximately one million dollars. Originally, in that 9-month timeframe, we had over 30 days of available slack time. But as we finished the planning process and began the execution phase, I started to receive change requests. Using the principles I describe in this book, I worked each change request through the change request process that I had created. I was very careful about only getting change requests approved that could fit into the appropriate slack time.

After two months, I had approved 5 change requests and had absorbed 17 slack days. I was pretty pleased that we would be able to complete the project on time and still accommodate some of the change requests.

However, around the same time that the change requests started coming in, I noticed that multiple tasks were starting to slip. I did my usual variance analysis and did what I could to get the project back on track. This slippage continued over the next month. Every week I worked the issues to get the project back on track. I knew the time available was sufficient to cover both the regular work as well as the change requests. However, when everything was said and done, my project delivered three months late with a budget overrun of more than $150,000.

With lessons learned meetings and a lot of analysis, I realized that my project got hit with what I call the incremental effect. So what is this thing called the incremental effect? Well, it's made up of several theories: the theory of disruptions, including all of the starts and stops that result from change requests; the theory of timing; and the theory of not taking any of those factors (disruptions, the timing of the change requests, and the starts and stops) into account in your estimating process.

In Chapter 4, I talk about how to keep the team focused. Well, sometimes no matter what you do to keep the team focused, the incremental effect still takes over. The sheer number of change requests coming in can throw your project off track because they all distract you from the real project work. In addition, the number of starts and stops that result from dealing with these change requests throws the project off track. Let's spend some time talking about each of these theories and also about possible solutions.

The Theory of Disruptions

When you manage your change request system, you rely on your core team and/or team leaders to analyze each change request that comes along. You need each of these people to do their analysis because they are the ones who will coordinate the change for that part of your project team. Human behavior also dictates that you ask the person doing the work to do the estimate. When you include people in the estimating process, they are more likely to take ownership of the estimate. For instance, if someone tells you a task is going to take five days, they are apt to try their hardest to be done in five days.

Disruptions to the project result from change requests. Every time a change request comes along, the core team must stop the forward motion of the project to analyze the request. The forward motion stops, they do some analysis, they do a little more work on the project while they wait for an answer, they fret about the change request, they do a little more work on the project, they hear a rumor about the change request, so they talk to their fellow team members for an hour about the politics of the change request, and so on. Before you know it, you've only gotten four hours of work done this week on the project and four hours on the change request; you've lost 32 hours to the disruption.

So you have the following dilemma: The people who are working on the project are also the people who must analyze the change requests. How do you get everything done and still keep the project on track? Here are some things you can do to manage the results of this theory of disruptions.

Evaluating Change Requests Before Giving Them to the Team

Let's add a couple of steps to the change management process you designed in the previous chapters. These steps basically provide a filtering activity the project manager performs, as depicted in Figure 5.1.

FIGURE 5.1: Filtering a change request

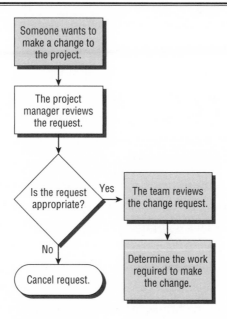

The project manager is the first person to review the change request. They determine whether the request even warrants a review. In this situation, you need to use your negotiation skills to convince the requestor to either hold for a later date or cancel the request based on what you find. Here are some items that you need to consider while you are reviewing the change request.

Is it out of scope? To determine whether the change request is out of scope, take the original scope statement and compare the change request to the original scope. If the change request is not in scope, you may have some leverage with the requestor. Be sure to review who signed off on the project plan and the product requirements. Remember that if the requestor signed, this means they agreed that the requirements and project plan were good to go.

Why is this change needed? Look at who requested the change and why they want it. Try to determine if the product absolutely has to have this change. Review the established quality parameters for the project. Will the quality of the project be compromised if this change is not added?

Is this gold plating? *Gold plating* is a term used in the software development industry to mean you are making the product better than it needs to be. You need to review the change request with this concept in mind. By making this change would you be gold plating it?

Once you've done some analysis, you'll probably need some one-on-one time with the requestor to make sure you understand what they want. Before you schedule this meeting, make sure you have a strategy planned for how you want to handle this request. Your strategy depends on whether the change request is warranted or not warranted.

Warranted If the request is warranted, you need to determine when to apply this change request. As long as you use the product requirements you established for your project at the outset, you already have a clear objective that should be met within the timeframe of this project. When the project is complete, the product goes into some type of lifetime operations or maintenance. At this point, you will probably turn the product over to another department. If possible, try to time this change request so it occurs after your project has completed. For instance, your strategy may be to move the request to the next release of the product.

Another timing strategy you might employ involves asking for some additional funding to cover an additional phase of your project. Perhaps this change request can be performed after the initial release of the product.

Not Warranted If the request is not warranted, you need to convince the requestor to withdraw it. Use the answers to the previous three questions to make your case.

Regardless of whether the change is warranted or not, you also want to talk to the executive sponsor. As we saw in Chapter 4, the executive sponsor has the final say in your escalation process. Find out where your sponsor sits in relation to the change request. See if the sponsor has influence over the organization that is requesting the change; they may be able to get the organization to withdraw an unwarranted request or postpone a needed change.

With your analysis and strategy in hand, it's now time to meet with the requestor. Make sure this is a closed meeting for just the two of you. In this meeting, ask the requestor the same questions you asked yourself. You want to make sure you haven't assumed anything about the request that is invalid. Be sure to listen with an open mind. Hear what the requestor wants to do with the request. After all, this could be a project-saving change request; some fundamental flaw might be corrected with this change.

At this point in the meeting, you can probably decide whether this change is warranted. Here is where your negotiation skills come into play. Negotiate with the requestor until you can get to a win/win solution. If you have your ammo and negotiate well, the requestor should agree to your proposed solution and be okay with it. Remember, you really have nothing to lose with this negotiation other than your team's time. If you can't get to the win/win solution, agree to send the request through the change control process. If this change request is really unwarranted, it should end up being denied during the regular process. Using this strategy, you might be able to filter out a few of the requests before wasting the team's time. Your updated change management process should now look like Figure 5.2.

FIGURE 5.2: Updated change management process

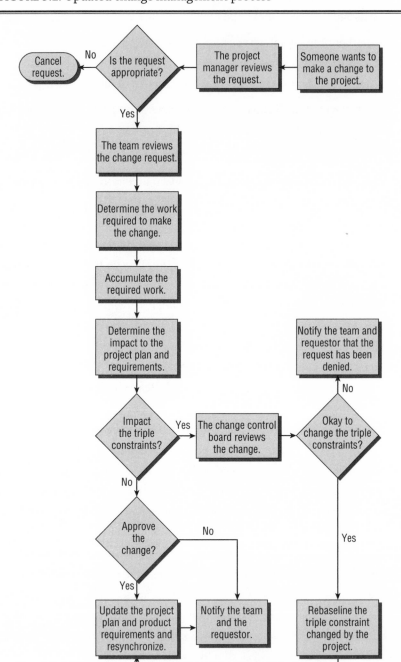

Scheduling the Core Team

When you originally planned the project and you allocated resources to each task, how did you schedule the core team? If you scheduled them just like any other resource, you may have created some problems for yourself. For instance, did you schedule the time they need for the change management process? If you didn't it's never too late to go back to your project schedule and build in the tasks your team needs to manage the change process.

This activity means *crashing* and *fast tracking* the tasks that the core team is scheduled to complete. Crashing involves removing some tasks from the critical path and finding a way to do them in a parallel workflow, thus reducing the duration of the critical path. Fast tracking is adding additional resources to tasks on the critical path to reduce the duration of the task. We know from Appendix C that if you reduce the duration of the critical path, you also shorten the entire project length. Figure 5.3 shows an example of using crashing and fast tracking to solve your scheduling problem.

In Figure 5.3, we have an old project schedule where Joe has several critical path activities that require his attention. In the new critical path, we fast tracked the tasks by asking Sam to work with Joe on a couple of tasks. Now that Sam is taking some of the work, Joe's change management analysis is no longer on the critical path.

Performing the change management analysis at the same time as the prototyping work is a crashing technique. This technique lets you use other resources to accomplish activities the core team was originally going to do, thus keeping the core team free to coordinate their subteams' activities as well as to perform the change control activities.

As long as we are on the subject of scheduling resources, what did you use as the length of a day in your project schedule? Most project managers do not bother resetting a typical day from the project management software's default of 8 hours. Ask yourself, "How do people normally work at this company?" Here are some things to consider when you are setting the working time default for the hours people will work on your schedule.

- Are there administrative items team members must do every day (i.e., reading email, attending status meetings, etc.)?

- What is the size of the team? If you have more people on the team, they require more administrative time.

- What is the complexity of the project? The more complex the project, the more time it takes to communicate and make sure everyone understands.

- How experienced is the team? The less experienced they are, the more communication and meeting time you will need.

- What is the availability of historical data? If you supply the team with information on similar, previous projects, the more productive they will be.

FIGURE 5.3: Crashing and fast tracking example

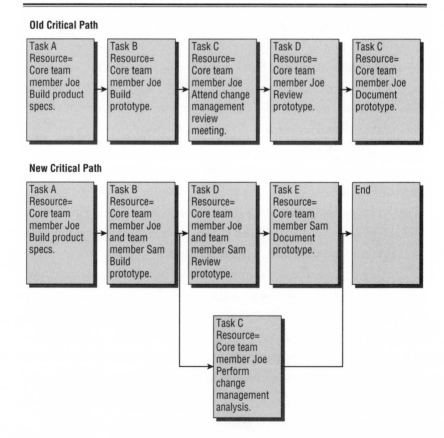

Take these questions into consideration to determine exactly how many hours a day a typical person is really productive. My guess is you'll find that most people are really only productive 4–6 hours per day, and you're kidding yourself if you think you're getting more than that worked on your project. If you want to reset the working day hours on your project management software, be sure to make a copy of your original plan first. Do this "what if" scenario on a copy. You want to analyze the effect this change makes on the end date of your project before you actually make the change on your working project schedule.

Delegating to Other Team Members

If you find that your core team members are too valuable to move away from doing regular project work and coordinating the subteam activities, you may want to consider delegating the change management chores to others on your team. You will still want your core team members involved a little, maybe as a final review step, but you can have another team member actually analyze the change and provide the information you need to determine whether the change should be done. However, please be aware that there's a lot of danger in taking this approach. If the junior person makes mistakes in analyzing the change request, you could have more problems than just scheduling issues.

Analyzing What's Prompting the Change Requests

One of the things that you might do to minimize the disruptions caused by change requests is evaluate the types of change requests that you're getting. You're really going to have to do a root cause analysis here to determine what is prompting the requests you're getting.

Are you getting lots of change requests that get halfway through the change management process and are then thrown out? If that's the case, you may have some fundamental communication problems. People may not understand what has been planned or what they have committed to for this project. Perhaps you should go back to your communication plan and beef it up. In addition to beefing up the communication plan, you might want to consider setting up a special meeting to walk the entire team back through the project's goals and objectives. You may have a situation where people simply just didn't get the concepts the first time around. You'll probably have to go back and recommunicate some of the things you thought were already complete.

Are you getting lots of change requests that want to change the fundamental product of the project? How many of these are you getting? How severe are the changes? If you are getting these types of requests, you may want to reevaluate your product design—perhaps it is flawed. Pull your experts together and figure out what it will take to get the product back on track. This may be an issue to take to the executive sponsor. It may be cheaper and faster to redo the product requirements and go back to the planning phase than to keep addressing the change requests one at a time. This may also be a situation in which the project's scope wasn't defined well enough. Just like the fundamental design, you may want to go back and rescope the project and, of course, recommunicate the new scope.

Are you getting lots of change requests that are frivolous and really shouldn't have been submitted at all? Again, evaluate the source of the change requests. Are they all coming from one area? Are they all coming from one person? Are these requests politically motivated? Dig back to the source and try to determine the motivation for these requests. You may need to work one-on-one with this person or organization to get them to stop sending the requests, or at least to understand the project better so that they only send in valid change requests. If you end up with this type of situation, you may have a case where people fear the change that the project is forcing on them.

Are the change requests coming from your own team toward the end of the project? This is what I call the 95-percent-complete syndrome. Sometimes team members don't want a project to end because they have some worries about their next assignment, as was the case in the "Change Management and Fear" sidebar. Part of your responsibility as a project manager is to be aware of the future position for each team member. Are they being

CHANGE MANAGEMENT AND FEAR

Fear is a great deterrent. I once worked on a project where this became obvious when the project was nearing completion. The trouble arose when we were in the process of finishing the last set of tests for the product. Every time we ran a test, the client said the product wasn't working right. Every time we evaluated the test results, we realized the client was wrong. We went round and round for a week or two with the client and couldn't get him to agree. The whole thing was just illogical. When we stepped back and analyzed the situation, we realized that this client was being transferred to another position as soon as the project was completed. We then took the time to conduct an orientation session for the client on his new job. Once he understood what his new job was going to be and began to feel more comfortable, he finally was able to sign off on the product testing.

let go? Are they moving to another project? Are they going back to their old functional area? You need to calm their fears of the future so the project can proceed to completion.

The whole point here with the theory of disruptions is *take action*. Don't sit back and just run your change management process and hope for the best. When lots of change requests come through and disrupt your project, you need to analyze what is happening and do something about it to keep your project on track.

The Theory of Timing

In Chapter 2, I talked about the importance of timing when it comes to setting up your change management process. Timing is also critical when dealing with the execution phase of the project. The critical point here is *when* you accept changes to your project.

Let's take a look at a typical project management lifecycle as depicted in Figure 5.4. As you might remember from Chapter 2, you need to plan and baseline your project schedule and product requirements before you begin the execution phase of the project management lifecycle. Let's now concentrate on the execution phase and how to handle change requests during this phase.

FIGURE 5.4: Project management lifecycle

Now you might think that all change requests are handled equally—well, they're not. As a result, some change requests are less desirable to implement than others. The more change requests you accept over the execution phase, the better chance you have of delaying the entire project. So what do you do to manage the timing of accepting change requests throughout the execution phase?

More at First, Less Over Time

Determine the total duration of the execution phase of your project. The execution phase should begin the day you baseline and run until the day you close the project. Knowing this, you can accept and review a few change requests at the beginning of the execution phase, as long as you have the slack time to cover them. As the execution phase continues, however, you will accept fewer and fewer change requests.

For example, say you are two weeks away from delivering your project's product. Someone sends in a change request to redo an important feature. If you accept this change request, it delays the entire project, just because so much of the work has already been completed. But if the same change request is presented at the beginning of the execution phase and completed with slack time, it might not delay the project at all.

Here's another example. Let's say you have a contractor painting your house, which has four external walls. The contractor is currently painting the first of the four exterior walls. If you change your mind now about the color, it is not that big of a deal. However, if you change your mind as he is starting the fourth wall, there's a good chance he won't finish on time.

No More Changes Date

Once you know the total duration of the execution phase, you should also set a "no more changes" date. At the beginning of the execution phase, announce this date to the entire team, clients, and executive sponsors. You'll want to set the "no more changes" date at the point in time that is right for you project. Ask yourself, "How much time will my team need to bring the project in if they don't have any more distractions?" For instance, for the example lifecycle in Figure 5.4, you might want to set the "no more changes" date for the end of the second month. This leaves your team with one good month to finish up the work. Your painting contractor would probably set the "no more changes" date for the day he begins painting.

Be aware that people will still bring you change requests after you set the "no more changes" date. You, the project manager, still need to review these changes and work closely with the requestor. However, at this stage, you will be forcing these changes into another project that will follow this one if possible. This solution allows you to get the first version out the door at least. You also may have a situation where the change request is completely warranted and really does need to be done in order for the product to be done right. If that's the case, you do need to take the request through the entire change process and the change control board. Obviously, this change will impact the triple constraints.

Now let's talk about the last theory of the incremental effect, the theory of estimating change requests.

The Theory of Estimating Change Requests

As you know, change requests are handled during the execution phase, which is really pretty late in the project game. Take a look at our project lifecycle in Figure 5.4 again. Execution comes after both the initiation and planning phases. You've already covered a lot of project ground by this point in time. The regular processes that you use to estimate tasks may not work in this phase, especially since there is so much potential risk in taking on additional tasks this late in the game. So what do you do to improve the estimating process for your change requests throughout the execution phase?

Increasing Your Estimates Using a Different Technique

Most project managers take the first estimate that a team member provides and use it as the estimate for any task on a project. This is because that first estimate is usually their best guess. As you are estimating your change requests, however, you might want to take a different tack. Instead of using the first estimate you're given, quiz your team members about a couple sets of different estimates. Ask them to provide an optimistic estimate. Ask them to base this estimate on everything going perfectly. This estimate should be smaller than the best guess estimate—usually people take some risks into account when they provide their first estimate. This first request gets them thinking and estimating differently. After they've provided you with their optimistic estimate, ask them to provide a pessimistic estimate. This estimate is based on everything going very wrong. You know, Murphy's Law is in full force and nothing is going right. This estimate should be much higher than the "best guess" estimate. Now, when it's time to evaluate the change request, be sure to use the pessimistic estimate. Chances are good that you will use every minute of the pessimistic estimate because of the stops, starts, and disruptions.

Picking a Percentage and Increasing It

Sometimes the easier way to increase an estimate is get the "best guess" estimate from the person doing the work. You can then determine how much of an increase is appropriate to add to the estimate. Most project managers use a percentage from 10–25 percent depending on how much risk is involved in doing this change request.

Regardless of which method you use, you need to consider adjusting your estimating process when you're dealing with change requests, especially when you're partway through the execution phase. There is too much to lose to not plan for the worst.

Case Study

Chris was feeling pretty good about the solution she devised for the sales training session. But that euphoria was short lived.

When Chris got back to her desk, she had noticed a revised agenda. She was very pleased with the team for keeping the work going but then noticed a facilitated team building session slotted for Thursday afternoon at a cost of $4000. This team building session was not discussed in the original agenda design session and the requirements didn't specify any. Chris wonders where this idea came from. She knows she can afford the team building session and that they have some slack hours available, but she wants to keep those slack hours and the little bit of extra money for emergencies. She has already talked to all of the team members about the change management system. How has this gotten on the agenda?

Chris knows she needs to nip this type of behavior in the bud. If she allows this one unauthorized change to get through, she could have a mess on her hands. Chris calls an emergency core team meeting to discuss the new agenda. She schedules it for later that day.

At the meeting, Chris asks the core team who added the new item to the agenda. Brian Gage mentions that Kelvin thinks it is a good idea to have a team building session because they have so much at stake with this new product. Chris asks Brian why he didn't go through the change management process that they all discussed. Brian says he thought of doing that, but that Kelvin told him not to bother because this was such a good idea. Chris reminds Brian of the team norms that they had all agreed upon. She tells the entire team that this is an unauthorized change and it will not be accepted. She also tells Brian she will be back to talk to him again later.

Next Chris calls Ruth and asks to see her for 15 minutes. Chris goes to Ruth's office and tells her that Kelvin and Brian decided to bypass the change management process. Ruth picks up the phone and asks Kelvin to come to her office. When Kelvin gets to Ruth's office, she tells him that bypassing the change management system is not appropriate. Ruth is holding Chris accountable for delivering this all hands meeting to the requirements that were laid out. She reminds Kelvin that he agreed to follow the process at the last staff meeting. She also tells him that complying with what has been agreed upon will be a future appraisal item. Ruth then calls each of her direct reports and makes sure they understand the importance of the change management system.

In the meeting, Ruth and Chris also agree that going forward, noncompliance at the team level means that the team member is thrown off of the core team. Chris goes back to Brian and explains to him that even though his boss told him to ignore the process, he still has to honor what the team agreed upon in the team norms. Chris advises him that if this happens again with Kelvin, he should refer Kelvin to Chris for resolution. Chris also tells him that he will be removed from the core team if he is responsible for any future problems with the team norms. After this discussion, Chris goes back to the core team and reiterates the team norms. She also lets everyone know that noncompliance with the team norms can result in someone being removed from the team. The entire core team definitely gets the message about the importance of the change management process.

That same week, Chris starts getting change requests through the normal process. Early that first week she gets three change requests. She approves two of them; together they take up 2 hours of her slack time and about $1000. She rejects the third. Friday she receives five more change requests. She decides that seven change requests the first week is pretty high and she had better analyze them to see what was going on. She asked the core team to continue making hotel arrangements and booking speakers while she does her analysis.

Chris reviews the change requests that are coming through and realizes that most of them have to do with meetings the executives want to have for their staff while they're in Las Vegas. They are basically taking advantage of the fact that they have their entire team together. She can't blame them for wanting to get as much done as they can during the session, but at the same time, they can't overspend her budget.

With this analysis, Chris decides to redo her communication plan. Evidently she was not clear enough on the ground rules for the all hands meeting. She immediately sends out a company-wide communication to reintroduce the project objectives and the parameters they are working under.

Chris also realizes that she needs to start padding her estimates for the change requests. Because the team has only estimated the cost of the speakers, the food, and the hotel, she isn't sure the team can stay within that overall project budget as they made their final selections. Any additional change requests that they decide to take on might throw them over budget. It is time to start being very pessimistic about any changes they are going to even think about taking on. Pessimistic also describes the approach that she uses to gather the estimates now.

Chris also decides that with one month to go until the all hands meeting, it was time to set up the "no more changes" date. She decides to allow another week for change requests, but then no more. She knows she had better get some communications out as soon as possible. With these decisions made, Chris returns to the five new change requests to begin their reviews.

CHAPTER 6

Change Tracking

In the last chapter, we spent a lot of time discussing how to handle multiple change requests and how they can incrementally impact your project more than you expect. In that chapter, I provided solutions for each type of incremental problem you might encounter when lots of change requests come your way.

By now, you've probably noticed that something is missing in our change management process—namely, how to track the changes that come through the process. In this chapter, I'll cover the tracking and paperwork you'll probably need to put into place to have a successful change management system. In addition to the paperwork, we'll also add a few more steps to our change management process.

Once again, I end the chapter with Chris Baxter and the all hands meeting project. We'll see how the incremental effect is jeopardizing Chris's project and whether she's able to successfully complete it.

Documenting a Change Request

When a change request is presented to a project manager, they need certain pieces of information to review the change and create an estimate for it. You'll want to create a form that requests the same information from each person who is asking for a change. The last thing you'll want to do is spend time chasing people around to get the information you need. We'll call this form a *change request form*. In the following sections, I talk about each piece of information you'll need. I've introduced an example throughout these sections. For each piece of information you'll see a paragraph explaining the piece of information and a second paragraph with an example.

Project Name

Each change request needs to identify the project for which the change is intended. Because your company may require that project managers manage multiple projects, identifying it in this manner provides a way to keep the changes straight.

For example, say you are the project manager at the Happy Toffee Candy Company. This year, for the holidays, the company has decided to introduce a new type of candy tailored specifically to the low-carb dieter. This is just one of the projects that you are managing right now. You've decided to give the project the same name as the new candy: Carbalicious.

Change Request Number (NO:)

Make sure to number each change request so it can be uniquely identified. One way to handle this is to use a sequential numbering scheme. Or you might decide to use something more meaningful to you, like the date and change number—for instance, you might use something like 100705-01, meaning the first change request received on October 7, 2005. Just make sure you design a numbering scheme that works for the information you need.

For example, for the Carbalicious project, you decide to number your change requests with the year, month, and day as well as a sequential number that depicts how many change requests you have received. Because the change request you just received is your third change request to date, you use 050914-03.

Date

Make sure you know the date on which each request is made. This information helps you make sure you handle each change request in a timely manner.

In our Carbalicious example, you document that you received this third change request on September 14, 2005.

Requestor

Make sure to note the person who is requesting the change. You need to make sure you send this person communications regarding the status of the change as well as the final disposition.

Let's see how this applies to our candy example. The primary chef at Happy Toffee Candy Company, Hank Stamp, who created the original recipe, is the requestor of the change. In the next section, you'll see that the change pertains to his original recipe.

Description of Request

The requestor should provide detailed information on the change that they are proposing. This detail should be robust enough for you and your team to take action without needing to have subsequent meetings to understand what the requestor wants. In order to get this type of detail, you might want to make a note on your form to request that additional documentation be attached. Make sure to encourage your requestors to provide this additional documentation as well as pertinent diagrams.

In the candy example, Hank's change request explains that he had to put together the original recipe for the new candy over the summer during the project feasibility stage. As a result, he felt rushed when he was developing the recipe. After the recipe was accepted and the project had moved into the development phase, he kept playing with the recipe to see if he could improve on it.

Hank states that he determined that the nut combination he was using with the mincemeat and sugar substitute was a little gummy. He just discovered that if you leave out the pistachios and substitute walnuts instead, the candy has a much better texture and is hoping to make this change part of the project. For accompanying documentation, Hank attached both the old and new recipe.

Reason for Request

You need to ask the requestor to provide information about why they think this request is important. Again, you want to make sure you get enough detail so that you understand the case they are presenting.

In his change request, Hank is pretty clear that the candy is much better with the walnuts than the pistachios. He talks a lot about the gumminess of the product prior to the substitution.

Risk if Not Implemented

Make sure the requestor understands that they should be clear in presenting their case for this change. They need to tell you what the ramifications of not making the change are as they see it. This information helps you make your decision on whether or not the change is warranted.

In the candy example, Hank states that the risk associated with not making the change is the potential loss of revenue.

In this example, the marketing department has already projected a revenue of over $1,500,000 if this product is good and hits the market by November 1, 2005.

Project Manager

Make sure you identify the project manager for the project. This could be important because your company might have one change control board that reviews all change requests for all projects. By specifying the project manager, you clarify who is accountable for getting this change reviewed and making sure its impacts are understood.

In our Carbalicious project, the project manager is Patty Burt. She is fairly experienced and handles most of the big projects at the Happy Toffee Candy Company.

Work Effort Required

After your team has had time to review the change, you'll use a field to document the team's findings regarding the work effort needed to make the requested change.

In the candy project, Patty and her team spend a lot of time reviewing this change request. Here is what they come up with:

- The development of the candy for the market trials is well underway. The market trials with focus groups is supposed to start in three weeks. To implement this change request, that development would have to stop and they would have to reeducate the staff on the new recipe. They anticipate the time they will need for this retraining to be two hours for four people.

- Creating the new candy would take three weeks. For the original development, there are two weeks remaining in the schedule. To make the change, they could use those two weeks and one additional week. Thus, they anticipate an additional five days for four people to implement this change.

- The candy wrappers for the field trial are pretty generic, so they don't need to change due to the ingredient substitution. However, the candy wrappers for the product launch do need to be redone. At this point, the design is already completed for these. To make such a change, Patty needs to get the graphic designer to make the necessary changes. The team anticipates that this will take one person four hours to complete.

With the analysis completed, Patti calculates six and a half days of work effort to implement the change.

Duration Required

You use this field to document the duration you will need to implement the change request. Again, you use the results from your team's analysis to complete this field.

In the candy example, Patty's team also reports the duration they need for each of the activities that to be performed to make the change. Here is what they report:

- Reeducate the staff on the new recipe. This will take five days because Carlo is on vacation until next week. They can't complete this task until Carlo gets back. Once the change request is approved, they plan to educate part of the staff Wednesday this week. Carlo gets back next Tuesday, so means the reeducation has a five-day duration.

- The duration for creating the new candy will also be five days.

- The duration for creating the new wrapper will be one day. Even though the graphic designer can complete her work in four hours, she still needs to get approval for her changes, which should take another four hours.

Therefore, the total duration for implementing this change is 11 days.

Resources Required

Here is where you document the resources you need to make the change. Be specific about the types of resources you need. In fact, it is even better if you can specify the exact people you need.

In our example, Patty easily determines the resources she needs to implement the change from the information the team provided. She needs

- The development staff
- The candy creation kitchen and machinery
- The graphic designer

Dependencies

Make sure your change request document has a place where you can document the dependencies for this change.

In the case of the candy recipe change, from some of our previous discussions, you should already be aware that this product change must be completed prior to the field trial. You don't want to take the old product into the field trial if this change is approved.

Additional Cost Required

Here you need to capture the additional costs your team needs to implement the change.

In our example, Patty is able to calculate the additional costs for the project using the information about the work effort required. Here is what she concludes:

- The development of the candy for the market trials is well underway. For this change to be implemented, that development has to stop and the staff has to be reeducated on the new recipe. This is projected to take two hours for four people. Because the development staff has a loaded rate of $100 per hour per person, the cost will be $800.

- Creating the new candy will take three weeks. Because there are two weeks remaining on the schedule for the original development, they will just need one additional week. For five days for four people, the cost will be $16,000.

- The candy wrappers for the field trial are pretty generic so they don't need to change as a result of the ingredient substitution. However, the candy wrappers for the product launch do need to be redone. Because the design is already completed, Patty has to ask the graphic designer make the necessary changes. This will take the graphic designer four hours. The graphic designer is an independent consultant who charges $75 per hour. Therefore, the cost for the design change will be $300.

With the analysis completed, Patti calculates the total cost of the change request to be $17,100.

Risk if Implemented

Earlier, I talked about a field on your change request form that described the risks associated with not making the change request. In this field, you describe the risk associated with making the change. This is part of the analysis your team completes as they review the change request.

For example, Patty and her team talk a lot about the implications of making this change while they are analyzing all the ins and outs of it. After they finish their analysis, they feel that the major risk is not making the November 1 candy delivery date if this change is approved.

Triple Constraints Impacted

You use this field to describe the impact of the requested change on the triple constraints. In this field, you'll talk about each and every impact to the triple constraints of time, cost, and defined quality.

In the Carbolicious project, there is no slack time available in the critical path. If this change is approved, the project won't be able to deliver the candy to the market until November 7. Therefore, the triple constraint of time is affected by this change.

Contracts Impacted

Here you document whether the requested change creates a change to any existing contracts that pertain to this project. You use this information as input into your contract administration process, using it to manage, control, and change contract language as necessary.

For example, in the candy project, the graphic designer has a time and material contract with a "not to exceed" amount. This change request puts the contract over the amount. As a result, a new task order needs to be created because of this change.

PM Recommendation

The project manager uses this field to document their findings and provide a recommended disposition for each change request. Make sure they present enough detail to adequately describe why the change is being approved or denied.

As part of her due diligence, Patty decides to try the candy with the pistachios removed. She has to agree with Hank that the product really is better with the walnuts. She knows the company has a better chance of making their revenue projections with the better product. Therefore, Patty decides to recommend that the change be accepted even though it will cause the end date to be extended.

Signed PM and Date

The project manager signs and dates the change request form.

Change Control Board Recommendation

Back in Chapter 4, we decided that if a change request impacts the triple constraints, we need to ask the change control board to approve it. Here is where you document their decision regarding their recommendation.

Patty has done her homework. She makes sure that the change control board has a chance to taste the new product. They determine that a slight revenue reduction resulting from a late entry into the market is better than no revenue because of a lousy product. They approve the change request.

Signed Executive Sponsor and Date

The executive sponsor signs and dates the form on behalf of the change control board.

Joe Williams, the EVP of Happy Toffee Candy Company, signed on behalf of the change control board.

Disposition

The final disposition of the change request is noted here. The disposition covers whether the change was approved or denied.

For our example, we'll mark the box showing the change is approved.

Included in Version/Date

If the change request is approved, use this final field to verify that the change is actually put into the product of the project.

Continuing with our candy company example, we note here that the change request was applied to the second version of the product on 9/18/05.

Change Request Timing

The fields you decide to provide in your change request form tell the entire story of the change. The story begins on the day it is requested and ends the day it is denied or approved and the product of the project is modified because of the change. Because the change request form tells the entire story, you can see that the form lends itself to different periods of time:

1. When the change is requested

2. When the analysis is completed

3. When the disposition is known

With that in mind, gather the fields into different sections that represent the different stages of the change request. The example of a change request form in Figure 6.1 covers our Carbalicious project. For a blank change request form, refer to Appendix B.

In Figure 6.1, the requestor fills in Section 1. The project manager completes Section 2 after completing all of the analysis. The project manager also completes Section 3 and includes the recommendation from the change control board if one is needed as well as the final disposition of the change request.

Logistics

You want to help people use your change management system. You don't want people using the excuse that they couldn't find the change request form and that's why they didn't bother to use it. Put the blank change request form on a central server, project website, or other convenient place where anyone can get a copy. I always keep a stack of them on the project conference room table for easy access.

FIGURE 6.1: Change request form

Happy Toffee Candy Company

			NO: 091405-03
Section 1: Requestor Completes			
Project Name:	Carbalicious Project	**Date:**	091405
Requestor:	Hank Stamp		
Project Manager:	Patty Burt		
Description of Request:	Remove the pistachios from the Carbalicious candy. Replace the pistachios with walnuts instead.		
Reason for Request:	The original recipe called for pistachios as part of the nut combination. This original recipe was gummy in texture. I have continued to work with the recipe. The product loses its gummy texture with the substitution of the walnuts for the pistachios.		
Risk if Not Implemented:	The risk associated with not making the change will be lost revenue. The marketing department has already projected a revenue of over $1.5M if this product is good and hits the market by November 1, 2005. Without this change, the product won't be good.		
Section 2: Project Manager Completes			
Work Effort Required:	6.5 days	**Duration Required:**	11 days
Resources Required:	* The development staff * The candy creation kitchen and machinery * The graphic designer	**Dependencies:**	This change must be in place prior to the field trial.
Additional Cost Required:	$17,100	**Contracts Impacted:**	Graphic designer will need a new task order.
Risk if Implemented:	The major risk is not making the November 1 candy delivery date if this change is approved.		
Triple Constraints Impacted:	The project will deliver the candy to the market on November 7. The triple constraint of time is impacted because of this change.		
PM Recommendation:	The product is better with the recipe change. I approve this change even with the end date extension.		
Signed PM:	Patty Burt	**Date:**	Sept. 16, 2005
Section 3: Executive Sponsor Completes/CCB			
CCB Recommendation:	Approved. Revenue figures will be revamped because of late entry into the market.		
Signed Executive Sponsor:	Joe Williams EVP	**Date:**	Sept. 17, 2005
Disposition:	**Denied** [ ] **Approved** [X]	**Included in Version/Date:**	Version 2/9-18-05

You might want to provide a set of instructions with the form itself. Be sure to cover how the users should get the form back to you. Select a way that is easiest for your company. If you're still using quite a lot of paper, make sure you have an in-box that's labeled "Change Requests." If your company is into email, ask your IT group to set up a special email account like "abcprojectchangerequests@xyzcompany.com" or at least make sure that the instruction set includes your email address.

One more thing about the logistics of a change request—make sure that you acknowledge its receipt. You want the requestor to know that you've seen the request and that you are beginning the process of review and analysis.

Recording information and providing logistics for your change requests are some of the things you'll need to do to document your change requests. The other important aspect is tracking the disposition of change requests.

Making a Change Request Log

Okay, it's Wednesday, and you received two change requests on Monday, one on Tuesday, and so far today, you've received two more. With all of this paperwork flying around, how are you going to keep straight where in the process each change request is?

You can accomplish this using a change request log—a simple mechanism for keeping track of each change. Pick a medium that is right for you, whether it is paper, a mechanized spreadsheet, a simple database, or something else, and create a change request log.

This log should summarize the information on each of your change request forms with enough information for you to be able to tell the status of each change with just a glance. You'll also use this log at the end of the project as an input into your lessons learned process. You'll review this log to determine what went right and what went wrong on your change management process. It also comes in handy when you start your next similar project because it quickly provides you with a review of potential risks to avoid. Here are some of the fields that you might consider putting on your change request log.

Change Number, Description of Change, Date Rcvd, Requested By
These fields are taken directly from our change request form.

Analysis Start Date You need to keep track of the date on which your team began the analysis of the impacts of the change request. Keeping track of this date also lets you know how long you're keeping change requests before you involve the team. Remember, you want to get through these things with minimal impact on the team as well as yourself. Don't put off getting them done.

PM Recommendation If you have decided not to pass the change request to your team, you need to document that recommendation here. You also use this field to document the team's analysis and your decision based on that analysis.

Disposition Here you document whether the change was approved or denied as well as the date on which the disposition was completed. Keeping this date again gives you an idea of how long a change request takes to get through the entire process.

Approved By This field explains whether the change request was settled by you, the project manager, or by the change control board.

Work Effort Populate this field with the work effort information from the change request form.

Cost Use the additional costs from the change request form to populate this field.

Resynchronize? Use this field as a reminder to go back and resynchronize your project plan and requirements if this change request is approved.

Included in Product Date This last field acts as a final check to guarantee that the change request was included in the product.

When your log is active, you'll be able to tell at a glance exactly where every change request is in the process. You'll also be able to quickly tabulate how many change requests are being worked as well as the additional costs and work effort. By scanning these fields, you can keep an eye on whether the incremental effect is starting on your project. I've provided a sample log in Table 6.1 as well as in Appendix B.

TABLE 6.1: Change management log

CHANGE NO: AND DATE RECEIVED	DESCRIPTION OF CHANGE	REQUESTED BY	ANALYSIS START DATE AND PM RECOMMENDATION	DISPOSITION DATE AND AND APPROVED BY	WORK EFFORT	COST	RESYNCHRONIZE? INCLUDED IN PRODUCT DATE
091405-01	Change name of product	Joe Williams	9/14/05 deny	Deny 09/14/05 PM	35 days	$55,000	
091405-02	Change inner wrapping	Sue Shelby	9/14/05 deny	Deny 09/20/05 CCB	14 days	$35,000	
091405-03	Recipe change	Hank Stamp	9/14/05 approve	Approve 09/17/05 CCB	6.5 days	$17,100	Yes Version 2 9/20/05

Finishing Up

You've now completed the documentation you need to manage a sound change management system. You have a change request form and a log to help you manage everything. Now all you have to do is add these steps to your change management system process flow. Here are these two new steps:

1. The requestor documents the change on a change request form.

2. The project manager receives the request and logs it.

These two new steps are depicted in Figure 6.2, and I have inserted them into the beginning of our change management process. However, you will need to continue to update your log throughout the entire time a change request is active.

FIGURE 6.2: New steps in the change management process

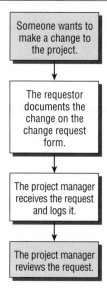

With the addition of these two new steps you have completed the change management process. You can see the completed process in Figure 6.3.

FIGURE 6.3: Complete change process

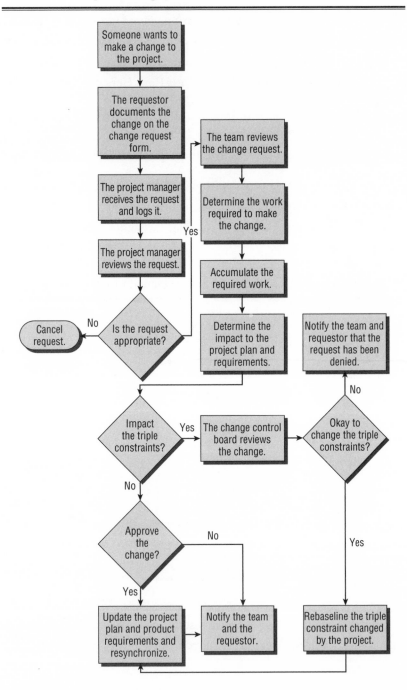

With this completed process and the tools described in this book, you will be able to control your project to guarantee a successful completion. Just remember to plan your change process while planning the project, communicating your expectations, and holding people accountable. And always, communicate, communicate, communicate.

Be sure you archive your change management logs as part of the project documentation to keep for future reference. Also, if you have changes that need to be implemented in a future version of the product, make sure those get covered in the scope statement of that future project. Always follow through with the commitments that you made.

Remember, there is a mysterious element that affects every project and yet is sometimes not planned for. What is this phenomenon? Some call it Murphy's Law. Some call it scope creep. Some call it change. Whatever you call it, you can employ tools and techniques that will help you manage it and benefit your project at the same time. I hope that this book has given you the ins and outs of successful change management.

Let's now see if Chris Baxter can hold on and get the all hands meeting completed on time and on budget.

Case Study

The last time we talked to Chris Baxter, she had just redone her project communication plan because she realized the amount of change requests that were coming in was high. She was aware of the incremental effect and started taking action to correct the problems she was starting to see.

In addition, Chris had dealt with the agenda change for the team building session that had been slipped in without following the team norms and change management process and she had made sure everyone was back on track. She did this by taking the agenda change and turning it into a change request; she then showed it as being denied. She knew the all hands meeting couldn't afford the team building session at a cost of $4000.

Now let's rejoin Chris. So far Chris has received three change requests earlier this week and five more today. She is pleased that the change request form she designed earlier is working well. In fact, she thinks it is working almost too well considering the number of change requests that are flying in the door. Chris also realizes that she is having a hard time keeping track of the changes, so she decides to utilize a change request log. The log for Chris's project is depicted in Table 6.2.

Chris knows that keeping the log will give her the ability to track the status of each change request. She also realizes that by using it, she will be able to tell exactly how much money and time is being added to the all hands meeting project.

Chris and the team dive into working on the five new change requests she has already received this week. She throws out one before the team even gets to see it. One staff member actually suggested that RemotesUS is a dysfunctional family and as a result, one of the guest speakers should be Dr Phil who would need to run a modified therapy session! Needless to say, a therapy session is not part of the requirements and Dr. Phil is most likely neither available nor affordable.

Because most of these change requests are coming in less than four weeks from the actual all hands meeting, the team provides pessimistic estimates for the other four change requests. Most of the agenda has already been set at this point, and it will be very difficult to accommodate any of these changes. As a matter of fact, Chris and the team only approve one of the four remaining changes.

Now that these four change requests are out of her way, Chris sends out a company-wide announcement that says that Friday is the "no more changes" date. She also sends out a copy of the proposed agenda at the same time. This allows the company to review the agenda and see if they have any more changes a couple of days before the "no more changes" date.

Thursday Chris receives one more change request. This last one is from Ruth requesting that the $1500 of the remaining all hands meeting budget be used for the rewards and recognition portion of the meeting. Ruth wants the $1500 converted into gift certificates. Chris and the team review the request and discover that even with pessimistic estimates, they think they can get this done in time to have the certificates at the meeting. This takes Chris's budget to $46,000. Chris is pleased that she still has a $4000 reserve for emergencies.

TABLE 6.2: Chris Baxter's change request log

CHANGE NUMBER AND DATE	DESCRIPTION OF CHANGE	REQUESTED BY	ANALYSIS START DATE AND PM RECOMMENDATION	DISPOSITION AND DATE AND APPROVED BY	WORK EFFORT	COST	RESYNCHRONIZE? INCLUDED IN PRODUCT DATE
1—9/10	Professional sales training	Craig	9/12—approved w modifications	Approved 9/13 PM	10 hours	$-500	Yes Y—9/15
2—9/15	Team building session	Kelvin	deny	Denied PM			
3—9/16	Troy party favors	Jennifer	9/16—approved	Approved 9/17 PM	1hour	$500	Yes Y—9/17
4—9/16	Change flight times for 5 employees	Craig	9/16—approved	Approved 9/18 PM	1 hour	$500	Yes Y—9/19
5—9/16	Helen of Troy costume for Ruth	Jennifer	9/16—deny	Denied PM			

Chris adds the change request to the project requirements and also adds tasks to the schedule to get the gift certificates. She then reviews the requirements and the project plan to validate that they are still in sync. Chris tells Ruth and the team that the change is approved.

The last three weeks of the project are a whirlwind of activity as the team works on last-minute details. They work with the catering staff to prepare meal selection. They have a last-minute cancellation from a motivational speaker. You know the drill, but finally it is the Tuesday night before the meeting and everyone is headed for the airport.

The next day, Ruth opens the meeting with a rousing speech about what the company has accomplished to date and where they are going in the future. Right after she finishes her speech, a huge Trojan horse is rolled into the meeting room with a new remote for each employee inside. Ruth tells the company that RemotesUS is the Trojan horse that is going to take over the remote market in the U.S. with this device. The rest of the all hands meeting continues with the Trojan horse theme. Chris hates these types of theatrics, but she decided to acquiesce to what the rest of the core team thought would be motivational and appropriate. The idea for the horse came from the sales team (of course) who saw themselves as the conquering heroes.

The meeting continues pretty much as the team planned. The only thing they forgot was to ask about dietary restrictions for the employees. As a result, several folks could not eat the food they planned for. Chris has to make last-minute arrangements with the kitchen for these special meals. When she gets the hotel bill later, she discovers that they charged her an additional $1100 for these last-minute meals.

The all hands meeting is scheduled to end at 5 p.m. on Friday for everyone except the sales team who, of course, are staying over for their sales training on Saturday. The last event on the agenda on Friday at 4 p.m. is the rewards and recognition session. Each executive gets up on stage and recognizes their exceptional performers. Some people receive checks, some receive gift certificates, and others are just acknowledged. The last person to make a presentation is Ruth who asks Chris and her core team to come on stage and receive gift certificates for their work on the all hands meeting. Each core team member gets a gift certificate for $250. Chris gets one for $500. More importantly, Ruth tells the company that the way Chris handled her project management responsibilities is what she expects of all project managers going forward. Needless to say, Chris is thrilled with the acknowledgment.

After everyone gets back to the office on Monday, Chris pulls the core team together for a lessons learned session. They identify what worked and what didn't. They document each of the items for future reference. They analyze the change request log and realize that even after replanning the project communications, they really didn't do a very got job of keeping the company informed about the project. Most of the change requests are based on people asking for things that weren't in the project's scope. Perhaps they should have done a better job of making sure everyone knew the scope? All in all though, the event was a success. They met all of the requirements and kept the event to three business days and a total budget of $47,100. The surveys the rest of the company filled out after the meeting also contained glowing reports.

That night Chris reflects back on the project and realizes that it was much more demanding then she originally thought. She is pleased that she did not blown off the fact that the all hands meeting was a project and therefore really needed the appropriate amount of rigor applied to it. Chris also realizes that she has lots of project management tools and techniques. She knows that selecting the right ones to apply to any project is really what good project management is all about. She is very glad that she applied a strong change management system to this one!

Nine Knowledge Areas Refresher

This appendix is a crash course on *A Guide to the PMBOK*'s project management process groups and the nine knowledge areas. All projects progress through a logical series of steps, starting with the initiation of a project all the way through to the ending, or closing, of the project. The information in this appendix will describe each of these processes along with the types of results or outcomes you're likely to see from each.

Following the process groups discussion, you'll find the nine knowledge areas. These describe the types of information and knowledge project managers must have to successfully run projects. Each knowledge area lists the project management processes found within that discipline, according to the 2000 and 2004 versions of *A Guide to the PMBOK*. Every four years, the Project Management Institute (PMI) modifies and enhances *A Guide to the PMBOK*. Changes reflect new information, industry trends, and best practices. Since the Spotlight Series spans both the 2000 and 2004 versions, you'll find both process listings in this appendix.

Project Management Process Groups

A Guide to the PMBOK describes and organizes the work of a project into five process groups: Initiating, Planning, Executing, Monitoring and Controlling, and Closing. Each group is interrelated and depends on the other. For example, you can't start the work of the project (Executing) without first initiating the project and creating a project plan—unless, of course, you work in Information Technology (IT) where we like to program the new system before we ask for requirements and then wonder why the end user doesn't like what we've done. (I trust all you great project managers out there are changing this paradigm.)

These process groups are iterative, meaning you might make several passes through each one throughout the course of the project. For example, changes might occur as a result of measurements you've taken (during the Monitoring and Controlling process) that require you go back to the Planning process and rework the schedule of some other part of the project plan. Risk management is iterative as well and should be performed throughout the life of the project.

Initiating

Initiating is the beginning process for all projects. This is where you decide whether to undertake the project by examining the costs and benefits of the project to the organization. It may also include an analysis of one project versus another project. For example, should you research and market a new product or consolidate the offices so all employees work under one roof? In the end, the Initiating process results in one of two decisions for each project considered—go or no go. Provided the answer is go, resources are committed to the project.

NOTE   Initiation is the formal recognition that a project, or the next phase in an existing project, should begin.

Some of the results produced during the Initiating process include the following:

- Defining the goals and objectives of the project
- Evaluating and determining project benefits
- Selecting projects based on criteria defined by a selection committee
- Writing the project charter
- Assigning the project manager
- Obtaining sign-off of the project charter

Planning

The Planning processes are the heart of all successful projects. And proper planning techniques can be the difference between a failed project and a successful one. This process outlines what's involved in completing the work of the project, where you're going, and how you're going to get there. As you probably already know, this process can consume a large amount of the overall project time, but it's well worth the investment.

Project planning involves researching, communicating, and documenting—and lots of it. What you do here will determine how the project will progress through the remaining processes. It also establishes the foundation for the rest of the project. If you communicate well with the stakeholders through this process, assure that all project team members and stakeholders understand the purpose of the project and how the work will be carried out, and establish a professional decorum with everyone involved, the stakeholders will feel confident that the project will be successful. You're also more likely to gain their cooperation later in the project when the problems start to appear.

Some of the results produced during Planning include the following:

- Determining project deliverables and milestones
- Writing and publishing a scope statement
- Determining requirements
- Breaking down the work of the project into tasks and creating a Work Breakdown Structure (WBS)
- Developing a project schedule
- Establishing a project budget
- Developing risk, communication, quality, and change management plans
- Determining resource needs
- Assessing special skills needed for project tasks and identifying resources
- Setting the stage for project success

NOTE   The Planning group is the largest of all the process groups. The project plans created here are the road map for achieving the goals the project was undertaken to address.

Executing

While the Planning process is the heart of determining project success, the Executing process is where the real work of the project actually happens. Great plans require follow-through, and this is what you do in the Executing process group.

In the Executing process you'll put all the project plans you've developed into action. Project team members complete the tasks. You keep the project team focused on the work of the project, and you communicate project progress to stakeholders and management. Once the work of the project begins, sometimes you'll need to change the project plan. It's the project manager's responsibility to update the project planning documents and redirect and refocus the project team on the correct tasks.

The Executing process is where you'll likely utilize the majority of project resources, spend most of the project budget, and run into scheduling conflicts.

Some of the results produced during the Executing process include the following:

- Obtaining project resources
- Establishing the project team
- Directing and leading the project team
- Conducting project status meetings
- Publishing project status reports and other project information
- Communicating project information
- Managing and directing contractors
- Managing project progress
- Implementing quality assurance procedures

Monitoring and Controlling

This group of project management processes involves monitoring the work of the project and taking performance measures to assure that the work performed is on track with the project scope and that the deliverables are being met. If performance checks during this process show that the project has veered off course, corrective action is required to realign the work of the project with the project goals.

Corrections and changes during this process may require a trip back through the Planning and Executing processes. Most often this will occur for one of two reasons—change requests or corrective actions.

Some of the results produced during the Monitoring and Controlling process include the following:

- Measuring performance and comparing to project plan
- Ensuring that the project progresses according to plan
- Taking corrective action when measures are outside limits
- Evaluating the effectiveness of corrective actions
- Reviewing and implementing change requests
- Updating the project plan to conform with change requests

Closing

The Closing process is the one project managers tend to skip. Once the project at hand is complete, it's easy to start focusing on the next one. Who wants to obtain sign-off, document lessons learned, and close out a project that's complete and that stakeholders love? You should.

One of the most important aspects of this process is documenting lessons learned. You and your project team have just completed a successful project where some processes worked very well and others could have been improved. Now is the time to capture the good and the bad so that the next project you (or another project manager in your company) undertake capitalizes on the lessons learned during this project.

Another aspect of this process is celebrating. Your team has met or exceeded the agreed-upon project goals, and the stakeholders are satisfied. That spells success, and success should be celebrated. Projects are truly team efforts, and it's always appropriate to congratulate your team on a job well done.

Some of the results produced during the Closing process include the following:

- Obtaining acceptance of project deliverables
- Securing sign-off from all stakeholders
- Documenting lessons learned
- Archiving project records
- Formalizing the closure of the project
- Releasing project resources

Figure A.1 shows the interaction and iterative nature of these process groups. While all the process groups are iterative, you'll find that most interaction occurs between the Planning, Executing, and Controlling process groups.

FIGURE A.1: Project process groups

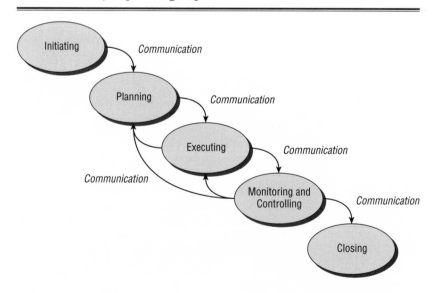

Project Management Knowledge Areas

According to *A Guide to the PMBOK*, nine knowledge areas comprise project management: Project Integration Management, Project Scope Management, Project Time Management, Project Cost Management, Project Quality Management, Project Human Resources Management, Project Communications Management, Project Risk Management, and Project Procurement Management. Each knowledge area deals with a specific aspect of project management such as scope management and time management. These areas consist of individual processes that have characteristics in common. For example, the Project Procurement Management knowledge area consists of processes dealing with procurement planning, solicitation, source selection, contract administration, and so on.

You should familiarize yourself with each knowledge area and the processes they include. They provide the foundation for solid project management practices.

If you'd like further information on these knowledge areas and their processes, pick up a copy of *PMP Project Management Professional Study Guide* by Kim Heldman.

The knowledge areas and a brief description of each follow.

Project Integration Management

The Project Integration Management knowledge area is concerned with coordinating all aspects of the project plan and is highly interactive. It involves project planning, project execution, and change control. All these processes occur throughout the life of the project and are repeated continuously while working on the project. Project planning, execution, and change control are tightly linked. The processes that constitute Project Integration Management include the following:

2000 PMBOK	2004 PMBOK
Project Plan Development	Develop Project Charter
Project Plan Execution	Develop Preliminary Project Scope

2000 PMBOK	2004 PMBOK
Integrated Change Control	Develop Project Management Plan
	Direct and Manage Project Execution
	Monitor and Control Project Work
	Integrated Change Control
	Close Project

Project Scope Management

The Project Scope Management knowledge area is concerned with defining all the work of the project and only the work required to complete the project. The processes involved in project scope management occur at least once during the life of the project and sometimes many times throughout the life of the project. For instance, Scope Planning entails defining and documenting the work of the project. Scope Change Control is the process that handles changes to the agreed-upon scope. Changes, as you probably guessed, require changes to the Scope Planning process, and thus the cycle perpetuates. The processes that constitute Project Scope Management include the following:

2000 PMBOK	2004 PMBOK
Initiation	Scope Planning
Scope Planning	Scope Definition
Scope Definition	Create WBS
Scope Verification	Scope Verification
Scope Change Control	Scope Control

Project Time Management

The Project Time Management knowledge area is concerned with setting the duration of the project plan activities, devising a project schedule, and monitoring and controlling deviations from the schedule. Time management is an important aspect of project management because it keeps the project activities on track and monitors those activities against the project plan to ensure the project is completed on time. The processes that constitute Project Time Management include the following:

2000 PMBOK	**2004 PMBOK**
Activity Definition	Activity Definition
Activity Sequencing	Activity Sequencing
Activity Duration Estimating	Activity Resource Estimating
Schedule Development	Activity Duration Estimating
Schedule Control	Schedule Development
	Schedule Control

Project Cost Management

As its name implies, the Project Cost Management knowledge area involves project costs and budgets. The activities in the Project Cost Management area establish estimates for costs and resources and keep watch over those costs to ensure that the project stays within the approved budget. The processes that make up Project Cost Management include the following:

2000 PMBOK	**2004 PMBOK**
Resource Planning	Cost Estimating
Cost Estimating	Cost Budgeting
Cost Budgeting	Cost Control
Cost Control	

Project Quality Management

Project Quality Management ensures that the project meets the requirements that the project was undertaken to produce. It focuses on product quality as well as the quality of the project management processes used during the project's life cycle. The processes in this knowledge area measure overall performance, monitor project results, and compare them to the quality standards. All this means the customer will receive the product or service they thought they purchased. The processes that constitute Project Quality Management include the following:

2000 PMBOK	2004 PMBOK
Quality Planning	Quality Planning
Quality Assurance	Perform Quality Assurance
Quality Control	Perform Quality Control

Project Human Resource Management

Ah, the people factor. Project activities don't perform themselves. It takes a village...no, that's someone else's line. It takes people to perform the activities of a project. The Project Human Resource Management knowledge area assures that the human resources assigned to the project are used in the most effective way possible. Some of the skills covered in this knowledge area include personal interaction, leading, coaching, conflict management, performance appraisals, and so on. The processes that constitute Project Human Resource Management include the following:

2000 PMBOK	2004 PMBOK
Organizational Planning	Human Resource Planning
Staff Acquisition	Acquire Project Team
Team Development	Develop Project Team
	Manage Project Team

Project Communications Management

The processes in this knowledge area are related to—you guessed it—communication skills. Communication encompasses much more than just a simple exchange of information. The Project Communications Management knowledge area ensures that all project information—including project plans, risk assessments, risk response plans, meeting notes, project status, and more—are collected, documented, distributed, and archived at appropriate times. Project managers use communication skills on a daily basis. According to some statistics (and most of you can attest to this from first-hand experience), project managers spend 90 percent of their time communicating. The processes that constitute Project Communications Management include the following:

2000 PMBOK	2004 PMBOK
Communication Planning	Communications Planning
Information Distribution	Information Distribution
Performance Reporting	Performance Reporting
Administrative Closure	Manage Stakeholders

Project Risk Management

The Project Risk Management knowledge area deals with identifying, analyzing, and planning for potential risks. This includes minimizing the likelihood of risk events occurring, minimizing risk consequences, and exploiting positive risks that may improve project performance or outcomes. The processes that constitute Project Risk Management include the following:

2000 PMBOK	2004 PMBOK
Risk Management Planning	Risk Management Planning
Risk Identification	Risk Identification
Qualitative Risk Analysis	Qualitative Risk Analysis
Quantitative Risk Analysis	Quantitative Risk Analysis
Risk Response Planning	Risk Response Planning
Risk Monitoring and Control	Risk Monitoring and Control

Project Procurement Management

The Project Procurement Management knowledge area concerns the purchasing of goods or services from external vendors, contractors, and suppliers. These processes deal with preparing requests for information from contractors, evaluating responses, and selecting the contractor to perform the work or supply the goods. It also deals with contract administration and contract closeout. The processes that constitute Project Procurement Management include the following:

2000 PMBOK	2004 PMBOK
Procurement Planning	Plan Purchases and Acquisitions
Solicitation Planning	Plan Contracting
Solicitation	Request Seller Responses
Source Selection	Select Sellers
Contract Administration	Contract Administration
Contract Closeout	Contract Closure

APPENDIX B

Change Management Templates

Your life as a project manager can be quite challenging at times. As you perfect your skills you find tools and techniques that work for you. You incorporate them into your project manager tool belt for use on your next project. I have provided here a set of templates for your future use. You'll also find them located at www.harborlightpress.com. I hope you find them to be great additions to your project management tool belt.

	Initiating	Planning	Executing	Controlling	Closing
Integration		1 planning process	1 executing process	Integrated Change Control T&T: Change Control System	
Scope	1 initiating process	2 planning processes		2 controlling processes, one that deals with change management: Scope Change Control T&T: Scope Change Control	
Time		4 planning processes		Schedule Control T&T: Schedule Change Control System	
Cost		3 planning processes		Cost Control T&T: Cost Change Control System	
Procurement		2 planning processes	3 executing processes		1 closing process
Quality		1 planning process	1 executing process	1 controlling process	
Human Resource		2 planning processes	1 executing process		
Communications		1 planning process	1 executing process	1 controlling process	1 closing process
Risk		5 planning processes		1 controlling process	

Change Request Form

				NO:
Section 1: Requestor Completes				
Project Name:		**Date:**		
Requestor:				
Project Manager:				
Description of Request:				
Reason for Request:				
Risk if not Implemented:				
Section 2: Project Manager Completes				
Work Effort Required:		**Duration Required:**		
Resources Required:		**Dependencies:**		
Additional Cost Required:		**Contracts Impacted:**		
Risk if Implemented:				
Triple Constraints Impacted:				
PM Recommendation:				
Signed PM:		**Date:**		
Section 3: Executive Sponsor Completes/CCB				
CCB Recommendation:				
Signed Executive Sponsor:		**Date:**		
Disposition:	Denied [ ] Approved [ ]	**Included in Version/Date:**		

Change Request Log

Change No. and date received	Description of Change	Requested By	Analysis start date and PM Recommendation	Disposition and date and approved by	Work Effort	Cost	Resynchronize? Included in Product date

Complete Change Process

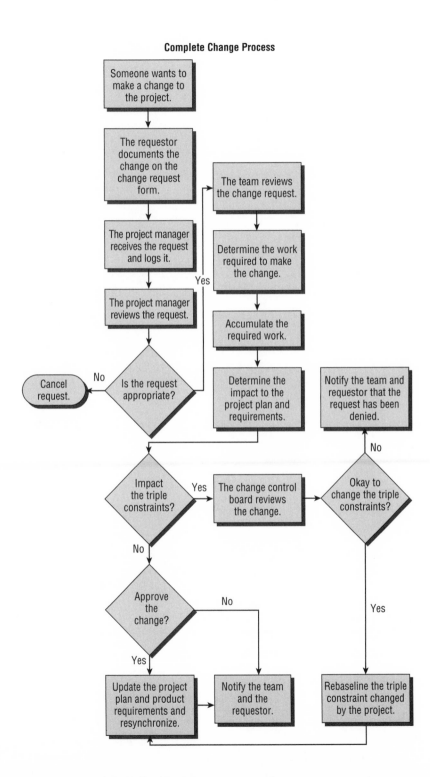

APPENDIX C

Calculating the Critical Path

I mention the critical path of a project several times during the course of this book. With this appendix, I provide a refresher course on how to determine the critical path for your project.

When you create a network diagram, you also create a critical path for your project. The *critical path* is the longest path through the project and has no float. The *PMBOK Guide* defines float as "the amount of time that an activity may be delayed from the early start without delaying the project finish date." When you look at your network diagram, the critical path and tasks with float may not be obvious. However, you'll want to learn how to manage the critical path, because if a task on the critical path slips, the end date of the project slips. To determine the critical path for your project, you use the Critical Path Method *(CPM)*, a tool and technique of the schedule development process called mathematical analysis as shown in the *PMBOK Guide*.

CPM helps you calculate a single critical path for the project. To get this result, you perform a forward pass, a backward pass, and calculate the float for the entire network diagram. The critical path calculation is done after the duration is known for each task.

In the remainder of this appendix, we'll calculate the critical path for the network diagram shown in Figure C.1.

FIGURE C.1: Network diagram

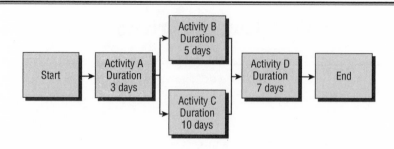

Performing a Forward Pass

Starting at the earliest point of the network diagram, a forward pass determines the early start and early finish for each task.

1. Start at the earliest point of the network diagram in Figure C.1 and look at Activity A. The earliest time it can start is day 0. Therefore the value for the early start is 0.

2. Now add the duration to the early start. The Early Finish is 3. $0 + 3 = 3$.

3. Continue through the network diagram and calculate the early start and early finish for each task.

4. When you get to Activity D, use the larger value for the early finish from either Activity B or C for the early start value of Activity D.

Activity	Early Start	Early Finish
A	0	3
B	3	8
C	3	13
D	13	20

Performing a Backward Pass

Starting at the latest point of the network diagram, a backward pass determines the late start and late finish for each task.

1. Start at the latest point of the network diagram in Figure C.1 and look at Activity D. The latest time it can finish is day 20. Recall that day 20 is also the early finish from the forward pass. Therefore the late finish is also 20. This is a rule of calculating the backward pass.

2. Now subtract the duration from the late finish to get the late start value. 20 – 7 = 13.

3. Continue through the network diagram and calculate the late start and late finish for each task.

4. When you get to Activity A, use the smaller late start value from either Activity B or Activity C to get the late finish of Activity A.

Activity	Early Start	Early Finish
D	13	20
C	3	13
B	8	13
A	0	3

Calculating Float

You calculate the float by subtracting the early start from the late start or by subtracting the early finish from the late finish.

1. Again start at the earliest point of the network diagram in Figure C.1 and look at Activity A. The late start value is 0 as is the early start.

2. Subtract the early start form the late start to get the float value. 0 – 0 = 0.

3. Continue through the network diagram and calculate the float for each task.

Activity	Float
A	0
B	5
C	0
D	0

If you look at the revised network diagram in Figure C.2, you can determine that the critical path is Activity A, C, and D. That's because none of these tasks has any float. In other words, the critical path has 0 float.

FIGURE C.2: Network diagram revised

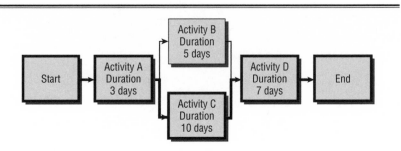

Reviewing the Critical Path Process

To review, here is how you calculate the critical path:

1. Take a look at the network diagram for your project.

2. Perform a forward pass by starting at the earliest point, day 0, and determining the early start and early finish for each task.

3. Perform a backward pass by starting at the latest point of the network diagram and determining the late start and late finish for each task.

4. Subtract the early start from the late start to determine the float.

5. Determine which tasks have 0 float. These tasks make up the critical path.

As you calculate the critical path for your project, you might notice that some of the paths on your network diagram have very little float available. These paths are sometimes referred to as near critical paths. As you manage the critical path, be sure to watch the near critical paths also. In this appendix's example, Activity B has 5 days of float available. If this task starts 5 days late, it also becomes the critical path for the project. Yes, a project can have more than one critical path. Any path through the network diagram with no float can be considered a critical path and must be watched closely.

L

Glossary

Baseline
A baseline of a project is a copy of what you planned to do so that you can use it for comparative purposes as you execute the project.

Change Control
The proactive identification and management of modifications to a project.

Change Control Board
A group of executives that are affected by the project who will make decisions regarding change requests that impact the triple constraints of time, cost, and quality.

Change Management
An overarching system that manages change with system meaning processes, forms, and possibly software.

Communicate
One of the fundamental activities of a project manager. Experts say this is 80–90 percent of a project manager's job.

Contract
A binding legal agreement that can be affected by changes in a project.

Control
Reviewing the project performance and taking action to manage any project variable that is not performing as expected.

Contingency Budget
Project money that is put aside to reduce the risk of project overruns.

Controlling Processes

One of the five process groups that is concerned with monitoring project performance and taking appropriate action to keep the project on course to deliver the project's goals.

Cost Baseline

The amount of money set at the end of the planning phase that the project will expend, by which actual expenditures will be compared, and deviations measured for management control.

Cost Control

Activities that ensure that changes to the cost of the project are managed.

Cost Management

The activities that manage the cost of the project from the original estimates through out the entire life of the project.

Crashing

Crashing is a technique used to compress the project schedule by decreasing the duration of the critical path. This can be accomplished by decreasing durations or adding additional personnel.

Critical Path

In a network diagram, the critical path is the longest path through the project. It controls the length of the project.

Escalation Process

An escalation process lines out exactly how decisions are made at every level of the project organization. It is commonly used when decisions at one level are questioned.

Fast Tracking

Fast tracking is a duration compression technique, which schedules activities in parallel that would normally be performed in a series thus reducing the length of the critical path.

Gold Plating
Making the product better than it is required to be.

Initiating
One of the five process groups that is concerned with establishing the project goals and officially commissioning work to begin on the project.

Leader
A person who is in a position that requires other people to follow their direction. Leaders establish direction and motivate and inspire others to achieve that direction.

Lifecycles
A series of stages or phases that something passes through during its lifetime.

Managerial Reserve
Additional project monies put aside to mitigate project risks.

Negotiating
A skill that requires communication in order to confer with another in order to come to terms or reach a mutual agreement.

Planning
The process of establishing activities that will carry out predefined goals.

Problem Solving
The ability to define the underlying cause of a dilemma and taking action to remedy it.

Product Development Lifecycle
A series of stages or phases that a product passes through during its creation.

Progressive Elaboration
Taking a concept and proceeding through a step-by-step method of detailing each aspect of the concept into explicit details.

Project Manager
The person assigned to a project by the performing organization who is accountable to achieve project objectives.

Project Management Lifecycle
A series of stages or phases that a project passes through during its lifetime.

Project Schedule
A series of tasks, dates, and milestones that depict the timetable of a project.

Resources
The items needed to perform project activities. Resources are people, materials (gas, water, electricity, etc.), or equipment (backhoe, printer, post-hole digger, etc).

Schedule Control
Activities that ensure that changes to the length of the project are managed.

Scope
The range of work that must be done to deliver the product of the project and only the product of the project.

Scope Statement
The formal document that describes the range of work that must be done to deliver the product of the project.

Slack Time
The amount of time that a task can be delayed without delaying the project end date.

Sponsors
People or organizations who have something to gain or lose depending upon the outcome of a project.

Time

The measurable period in which a project is planned.

Team Members

The people that work on a project.

Triple Constraints

The framework for evaluating the success of a project , such as on time, on budget, and built to the defined quality standards.

Index

Note to the reader: Throughout this index **boldfaced** page numbers indicate primary discussions of a topic. *Italicized* page numbers indicate illustrations.